Also by Adam Zagajewski

A Defense of Ardor

A Defense of Ardor Adam Zagajewski

Translated from the Polish by Clare Cavanagh Farrar, Straus and Giroux / New York

Farrar, Straus and Giroux
19 Union Square West, New York 10003

Distributed in Canada by Douglas & McIntyre Ltd.
Printed in the United States of America
Originally published in 2002 by Wydawnictwo a5, Poland, as *Obrona żarliwości*
Published in the United States by Farrar, Straus and Giroux
First American edition, 2004

Some of these essays previously appeared in *Common Knowledge, The New Republic, The Times Literary Supplement,* and the anthology *Planet on the Table* (Sarabande Books, 2003).

Grateful acknowledgment is made to HarperCollins Publishers, Inc., for permission to reprint the following previously published material:
Excerpt from "Mittelbergheim" in *New and Collected Poems*, by Czeslaw Milosz, translated by Czeslaw Milosz and Richard Lourie. English translation copyright © 2003, Czeslaw Milosz and Richard Lourie.
Excerpt from "Why the Classics" in *Selected Poems*, by Zbigniew Herbert, translated by Czeslaw Milosz and Peter Dale Scott. English translation copyright © 1968, Czeslaw Milosz and Peter Dale Scott.
Excerpt from "The Envoy of Mr. Cogito" in *Mr. Cogito*, by Zbigniew Herbert, translated by John and Bogdana Carpenter. English translation copyright © 1995, John and Bogdana Carpenter.

Library of Congress Cataloging-in-Publication Data
Zagajewski, Adam, 1945–
    [Obrona zarliwosci. English]
    A defense of ardor / Adam Zagajewski ; translated by Clare Cavanagh.
        p.   cm.
    ISBN-13: 978-0-374-13630-7
    ISBN-10: 0-374-13630-0 (alk. paper)
        I. Cavanagh, Clare. II. Title.

PG7185.A32O2413 2004
891.8'5473—dc22

2004053246

Designed by Jonathan D. Lippincott

www.fsgbooks.com

1   2   3   4   5   6   7   8   9   10

Contents

A Defense of Ardor

1 A Defense of Ardor

From Lvov to Gliwice, from Gliwice to Krakow, from Krakow to Berlin (for two years); then to Paris, for a long while, and from there to Houston every year for four months; then back to Krakow. My first trip was involuntary, forced by the international treaties that ended World War II. The second was simply the result of an ordinary thirst for education (back then young Poles thought that a good education could be found—if you looked for it—only in ancient Krakow). The impulse behind the third was curiosity about a different, Western world. The fourth was motivated by what we'll discreetly call "reasons of a personal nature." And finally, the fifth (Houston) was spurred both by curiosity (America) and by what might cautiously be termed economic necessity.

For over a hundred years Lvov had been the capital of Galicia, a province of the Hapsburg empire. It combined Western European cultural influences with an openness to Eastern emanations (though the East was certainly less obvious here than in Wilno or even Warsaw). Gliwice was once a provincial Prussian garrison town, with a history reaching back to medieval times. After the Second World War, the three elderly gentlemen ceded it to Poland. In school I learned Russian and Latin; I took private lessons in English and German. My family's—forcible—move from Lvov to Gliwice was symptomatic of a great change. Though it was in fact annexed to the Eastern empire in 1945, my country had paradoxically been shifted westward at the same time: the consequences of this shift would surface only later.

My grandfather was bilingual; Polish was his second language, since he had been raised by his dead mother's German family. But it never even occurred to him to claim *volksdeutsche* status during the Nazi occupation. As a young man he'd done a doctoral dissertation on Albrecht von Haller, which was written in German and published in Strasburg at the turn of the century.

In Krakow, I sensed the luminescence of all that was best in the Polish tradition: distant recollections of the Renaissance recorded in the architecture and museum exhibits, the liberalism of the nineteenth-century intelligentsia, the energy of the interwar period, the influence of the democratic opposition just then coming into being.

The West Berlin of the early eighties struck me as a peculiar synthesis of the old Prussian capital and a frivolous city fascinated by Manhattan and the avant-garde (sometimes I suspected that the local intellectuals and artists treated the wall as yet another invention of Marcel Duchamp). In Paris, I didn't encounter the great minds, the great French arbiters of civilization—I'd come too late for that. But I discovered nonetheless the beauty of one of the few European metropolises to possess the secret of eternal youth (even Baron Haussmann's barbarism hadn't ruined the continuity of the city's life). Finally, at this brief list's conclusion, I came to know Houston, sprawled on a plain, a city without history, a city of evergreen oaks, computers, highways, and crude oil (but also wonderful libraries and a splendid symphony).

After a time I understood that I could draw certain benefits both from the wartime disaster, the loss of my native city, and from my later wanderings—as long as I wasn't too lazy and learned the languages and literatures of my changing addresses. And so here I am, like a passenger on a small submarine that has not one periscope but four. One, the main one, is turned toward my native tradition. The other opens out onto German literature, its poetry, its (bygone) yearning for eternity. The third reveals the landscape of French culture, with its penetrating intelligence and Jansenist moralism. The fourth is aimed at Shakespeare, Keats, and Robert Lowell, the literature of specifics, passion, and conversation.

One August, the month when Europe relaxes intensively, we spent two weeks in one of its most beautiful landscapes, in Chianti, a part of Tuscany. A concert of chamber music was staged in the courtyard of a certain lordly manor, an eleventh-century monastery that hadn't held monks for centuries and had been transformed into a palace with a lovely garden. The audience for this concert was very distinctive, and consisted, with a few exceptions (one of them being the author of these words), of wealthy people possessing their own palaces, villas, and houses. This international company included a fair number of Englishmen (and also several Englishwomen who had decided for unknown reasons to behave like British clichés), a few Americans, and, of course, some Italians. In other words, the neighbors of the owner of this beautiful estate. Some of them only summered in Tuscany, others were full-time residents. The concert began with one of Mozart's early quartets; the four young women played wonderfully, but the applause was relatively sparse. I was a little annoyed and decided on the spot that it was time for a defense of ardor. Why couldn't the affluent audience appreciate this wonderful performance? Does wealth perhaps diminish our enthusiasm? Why didn't this ardent performance of Mozart meet with an equally ardent reception?

One of my vacation books at the time happened to be Thomas Mann's essays, including, among others, a piece called "Freud and the Future," a text written (and given as a lecture) in the thirties. What connection could there possibly be between the summer response of a rich crowd at a concert and Mann's essay? Perhaps only that I also found a rather summery, ironic attitude at work in Mann, who was searching for a new intellectual orientation while writing *Joseph and His Brothers*. It goes without saying that Mann's motivation had nothing in common with the blasé audience at an afternoon concert. In the essay, Mann interprets Freud's chief purpose as being something like the work of a sapper in a minefield: we're dealing with explosive materials of great force. Ancient myths conceal immense dangers; they're bombs that must be defused. Of course we need to read Mann's essays in historical perspective, recalling their context. The author of *Buddenbrooks* saw Nazism and fascism as a return to the energies of the mythic world, to the destructive violence of archaic myths, and hoped to resist this great wave of terror with the soothing substance of humanist irony. But this irony wasn't entirely defenseless, it wasn't simply abstract, "chamber" irony. It too was rooted in myth, but differently; it fostered life without recourse to violence.

Did Thomas Mann finally win? Since today, after all, we

hear rather similar tones within the most au courant, post-modern circles. Irony, it's true, has changed its meaning; it's no longer a weapon directed against the barbarism of a primitive system triumphing in the very heart of Europe. It expresses rather a disillusionment with the collapse of utopian expectations, an ideological crisis provoked by the erosion and discrediting of those visions that hoped to replace the traditional metaphysics of religious faith with eschatological political theories. More than one Eastern European poet employed irony as a desperate defense against barbarism—in this case, barbaric communism with its soulless bureaucracy (this time has passed —isn't neocapitalism an adroit ironist?).

But no, Thomas Mann didn't win, it was a different irony. In any case, we find ourselves in a very ironic and skeptical landscape; all my four periscopes reveal a similar image. The last bastions of a more assertive attitude stand guard perhaps only in my homeland.

Some authors flog consumerist society with the aid of irony; others continue to wage war against religion; still others do battle with the bourgeoisie. At times irony expresses something different—our flounderings in a pluralist society. And sometimes it simply conceals intellectual poverty. Since of course irony always comes in handy when we don't know what to do. We'll figure it out later.

Leszek Kolakowski also praised irony in his once-famous essay, "The Priest and the Fool" (1959). It really was famous, and not just in academic circles. It was avidly studied in Warsaw and Prague, in Sophia and Moscow, and probably in East Berlin. Brilliant and profound, it promised a new point of view. It called attention to the ubiquity, albeit in very contemporary disguise, of long-standing theological traditions. The dogmas of the hieratic priest—and every intelligent reader realized he was dealing with a passionate critique of Stalinism—were opposed by the behavior of the fool, quick-witted, shifty as Proteus, mocking a petrified civilization built on doctrine. Even today this essay still retains its freshness and the exceptional force of its reasoning. It marked a vital contribution to the critique of communist civilization; at the same time it arose from the moods of those times. In it we catch echoes of those countless, inspired, hilarious student cabarets that produced, in Gdansk, in Warsaw, in Krakow (and no doubt in other European cities seized by Moscow), a champagne of anti-Soviet humor. We also catch tones close to the "fool's" ontology in poetry (in Szymborska, for example, whose poems of that period should be read in concert with Kolakowski's programmatic essay).

Kolakowski distanced himself from his manifesto—his evolution reveals a growing fascination with theological issues (which had always intrigued him). Philosophy's splendid "technician," the author of *Main Currents of Marxism*, never ceases to approach faith asymptomatically, as if to say (not being a poet, he'll never just come out and say it) that you can't remain permanently in the fool's position, since its meaning is exhausted by its polemical attitude, its ceaseless needling of powerful opponents.

In a much later essay, "The Revenge of the Sacred in Secular Culture," Kolakowski writes, "A culture that loses its sense of 'sacrum,' loses its sense entirely."

The priest can get by without the fool; but no one's ever spotted a fool in the desert or a forest hermitage. Our epoch, though, that *puer aeternus* of history—worships perversity. It's no accident that Bakhtin's idea of the "carnival," the revolt against hierarchy, appeals so strongly to professors of literature.

In a section of *The Dehumanization of Art* eloquently entitled "Doomed to Irony," Ortega y Gasset points to the ironic character of twentieth-century avant-garde culture, its violent aversion to pathos and sublimity: "[T]his inevitable dash of irony . . . imparts to modern art a monotony which must exasperate patience itself."

Too long a stay in the world of irony and doubt awakens in us a yearning for different, more nutritious fare. We may get the urge to reread Diotima's classic speech in Plato's *Symposium*, the speech on the vertical wanderings of love. But it may also happen that an American student hearing this speech for the first time will say, "But Plato's such a sexist." Another student will note, on reading the first stanza of Hölderlin's "Bread and Wine," that in our great cities today we can't experience true darkness, true dusk, since our lamps, computers, and energies never shut down—as if he didn't want to see what really matters here, the transition from the day's frenzy to the meditation offered us by night, that "foreigner."

We're left with the impression that the present day favors only one stage of a certain ageless, endless journey. This journey is best described by a concept borrowed from Plato, *metaxu*, being "in between," in between our earth, our (so we suppose) comprehensible, concrete, material surroundings, and transcendence, mystery. *Metaxu* defines the situation of the human, a being who is incurably "en route." Simone Weil and Eric Voegelin (thinkers who loathed totalitarianism and from whom I first learned about Plato's *metaxu*) both drew upon this concept, albeit somewhat differently. Voegelin even made it one of the key points of his anthropology.

We'll never manage, after all, to settle permanently in transcendence once and for all. We'll never even fully learn its meaning. Diotima rightly urges us toward the beautiful, toward higher things, but no one will ever take up residence for good in alpine peaks, no one can pitch his tents there for long, no one will build a home on the eternal snows. We'll head back down daily (if only to sleep . . . since night has two faces. It is a "foreigner" summoning us to meditation, but it's also a time of absolute indifference, of sleep, and sleep demands that ecstasy be utterly extinguished). We'll always return to the quotidian: after experiencing an epiphany, writing a poem, we'll go to the kitchen and decide what to have for dinner; then we'll open the envelope holding the telephone bill. We'll move continuously from inspired Plato to sensible Aristotle . . . And this is as it should be, since otherwise lunacy lies in wait above and boredom down below.

We're always "in between" and our constant motion always betrays the other side in some way. Immersed in the quotidian, in the commonplace routines of practical life, we forget about transcendence. While edging toward divinity, we neglect the ordinary, the concrete, the specific, we turn our backs on the pebble that is the subject of Herbert's splendid poem, his hymn to stony, serene, sovereign presence.

But the connections between high and low are complex. Let's take a look at one of Chardin's still lifes, perhaps his beautiful *Still Life with Plums*, which hangs in the Frick Collection in New York: what we'll see is apparently only a tumbler made of thick glass, some gleaming enamelware, a plate, and a bulging bottle. Through them, though, we'll come to love singular, specific things. Why? Because they exist, they're indifferent, that is to say, incorruptible. We'll learn to value objectivity, faithful depictions, accurate accounts—in an age so adept at exploiting falsehoods, particularly in Central Europe.

Metaxu is something more than the state of being suspended between earth and heaven. For those who try to think and write, this category also holds a vital, double-edged warning. Since we can come to rest neither on the heights nor on the ground, we must keep close watch on our own selves and—if we seek a higher reality—guard against the rhetoric to which some pious persons fall prey. Religiosity may sometimes lead to insufferable self-assurance and thus produces, in a purely psychological (and linguistic) sense, the pompous cant to be heard in certain houses of worship. Although perhaps we shouldn't exaggerate. This is how the poet and philosopher Kathleen Raine deals with such accusations in her autobiographical book *The Land Unknown*: "Current morés have led to an increasingly radical overturning of the norms that dictate what should be said and what is best left unspoken. We think that admitting to base thoughts and deeds is more 'sincere,' hence more honest, than staying true to those perceptions that surface only when we step outside our ordinary 'I.' Bringing up visions of lofty, beautiful things is considered hypocritical self-glorification."

Wasn't Benedetto Croce also right in the talk he gave at Oxford in 1933, "The Defense of Poetry," when he commented that critics "are gifted with a strange immunity that permits them to spend a lifetime dealing with volumes of poetry, publishing them, appending footnotes, discussing various interpretations, studying sources, tracking down biographical information without the slightest risk of becoming personally infected with poetic fire"? He says something similar about priests: "[B]oth great minds and extremely simple people feel the call of religion, but not those who handle sacred vessels, not the priests and sacristans, who perform their rituals indifferently and at times without a trace of respect" (but not all priests surely!).

On the other hand, it's easy to "freeze" into irony and into a daily existence lived reflexively. This, I think, is the real danger of our historical moment, and not priestly pride (though we shouldn't overlook the dangers of religious fundamentalism). Moreover—though I may not be a neutral bystander here— ardor and irony are not symmetrically comparable. Only ardor is a primary building block in our literary constructions. Irony is, of course, indispensable, but it comes later, it is the "eternal fine-tuner," as Norwid called it; it is more like the windows and doors without which our buildings would be solid monuments, not habitable spaces. Irony knocks very useful holes into our walls, but without walls, it could perforate only nothingness.

We've learned to value things because they exist. In an age of lunatic ideologies, utopian nonsense, things endured in their small but stubborn dignity. This isn't all: we've also learned to value things because everything linked to them is distinct, sharp, definite. There's no haziness, no rhetoric, no excess. Since even Diotima from the *Symposium* may in her rapture veer off at any moment in the direction of pathos and—who knows—she may embarrass us. Our theologians—don't they eagerly abandon our sober shores, the territory where we can still follow them? Our Romantic poets, didn't they go a bit too far?

In effect, the students who try to diminish the sense both of Diotima's speech and of Hölderlin's opening stanza are defending themselves against pathos, as if they feared the devastating power of ecstatic experience; they're being nudged in that direction by the voice of that ironic prompter, our skeptical age. In this way, though, the marvelous *va-et-vient*, both archaic and contemporary, that negotiates between finitude and infinity, between sober empiricism and our intoxication with what's unseen, between our concrete, particular lives and divinity, is stopped short in its lower phase. This is not just the students' doing; they're joined by the majority of those who make pronouncements in print and on the Internet, our spiritual (or rather, intellectual) arbiters, our cultural leaders, our current *bien-pensants*.

Uncertainty doesn't contradict ardor. If we are to sustain the productive tension of *metaxu*, uncertainty (which is not the same thing as doubt!) will never be a foreign body, since our presence here and our faith can never receive absolute and permanent sanction, however much we long for it. Irony, on the other hand, undercuts uncertainty. When it occupies the central place in someone's thought, irony becomes a rather perverse form of certainty. Of course we can dig up dozens of uses for irony. In Zbigniew Herbert's poetry, to take one example, irony is ordinarily directed against the person passing judgment, the seeker of truth or law (the Greek Nomos), and often takes the form of self-irony. The truth-seeker views himself skeptically— "beware however of unnecessary pride/keep looking at your own clown's face in the mirror"—but not truth or law, as so often happens among contemporary authors, who happily cast doubt on everything but themselves.

We should remember, though, that in troubled times a move toward "beauty" may arise from an impure conscience, morally dubious circumstances. Thus in his stern essay "Der Schriftsteller Alfred Andersch," W. G. Sebald mocks Captain Ernst Jünger's raptures over Paris in flames: *Das brennende Paris, ein herrlicher Anblick!* (Burning Paris, what a sight!). Elsewhere in the same essay Sebald writes: "In *Kirschen der Freiheit* [Andersch's autobiography], discussions of the weekend flights into aesthetics that permitted the author to revel in Tiepolo's confectionary azures reveal once again his own lost soul."

Flights into aesthetics! I don't know Alfred Andersch's work well—he was a writer who struck a bargain with the Third Reich early on—but I think that Sebald may be right. (Certainly part—but not all!—of Jünger's own writing invites the same verdict.) Sebald doesn't quote another of Andersch's symptomatic pronouncements: "My answer to the totalitarian state was total introversion."

Anyone interested in the state of literature today should be aware that one of the paths leading to Platonic heights is the path of hypocrisy. At the same time, though, we can't overlook other roads that may be free of false piety. And the falsity of which Sebald accuses Andersch is most likely an ailment peculiar to totalitarian systems, and is thus unknown to Australians or Eskimos—or to the British poet I mentioned earlier, Kathleen Raine. Perhaps generations growing up today will know nothing of it. Beauty in the totalitarian state is a special problem. It is both Mandelstam in Voronezh yearning for Schubert and Ariosto, and the Polish poet Jaroslaw Iwaszkiewicz in Podkowa Lesna, the author of marvelous poems and a complete political opportunist. It's also the stanza of Dante in the camp at Auschwitz that Primo Levi describes. And Wat listening to Bach on the roof of the infamous Soviet Lubyanka. It seems that at least one crucial amendation is in order here: expeditions to "the heights" should be undertaken in a state of personal honesty.

And a sense of humor? Can it coexist with ardor? E. M. Cioran notes in his posthumously published diaries that "Simone Weil has no sense of humor. But if she had, she wouldn't have made such great strides in her spiritual life. Since a sense of humor keeps us from experiencing the absolute. Mysticism and humor are not on good terms." The next note in *Cahiers* modifies this observation, though; Cioran must have suspected that his comment was only half true and set about revising it: "Let us say that holiness can coexist with moments of humor and even irony. But it cannot tolerate systematic irony if it is to survive . . ."

And it's easy enough to imagine Meister Eckhart laughing, roaring with laughter. I don't see any fundamental contradiction between humor and mystical experience; both serve to wrench us out of our immediate, given reality. After all, our head tilts back in both a fit of laughter and a sudden influx of devotion!

Paul Claudel has a famous and beautiful sentence in the essay on Arthur Rimbaud that was published in 1912 in *La Nouvelle Revue Française*: "Arthur Rimbaud was a mystic in a savage state . . ." It might easily be used to describe all those poets who passionately seek a hidden truth. What's more, it works just as well for mystics. Since is it possible to imagine a domesticated mystic, a settled mystic, a mystic with a day job? A poet happy with his hunting? Sadly enough, we know firsthand how frequently one stumbles on complacent bards and self-satisfied theologians. But true quests are conducted, after all, only in a "savage state" . . . Claudel himself is a good example. His *Cinq grandes odes* hold marvelous, "wild" passages, while many of his later religious poems are marked by a far-reaching "domestication."

"We truly must have commited a crime that brought down curses upon us, since we've lost the whole poetry of the cosmos," Simone Weil says. Someone will object at this point: "Perhaps, but we've also gained something, we've become responsive to the misfortunes that befall both ourselves and those close to us, we've freed ourselves from the indifference that can afflict the devotees of poetry. More than this: we've become careful and critical observers of social reality." I don't want to make light of this: a critical stance (as long as it's free of Marx's dogmatic metaphysics) is exceptionally important, and if I speak here of the need for a different kind of quest, I don't want to be taken for someone who uses his religious concerns to repudiate social criticism. After all, Eastern Europe's former dissidents will never discount the importance of honest, courageous criticism of our social world—even if their own interests have evolved over time. We'd have to be idiots to forget this . . .

But what is poetry?

Anyone who looks through the catalogues of large libraries will find a fair number of variations upon the "defense of poetry." It's almost a separate literary genre, with its own venerable tradition (Philip Sidney, Shelley, and Benedetto Croce are among its classics). At the same time, though, it is a desperate genre, with something panic-stricken about it. The titles themselves, which struggle to convince us of poetry's "necessity," vitality, indispensability, sound nonetheless suspiciously close to capitulation. If you have to insist so strenuously . . . Authors like Joseph Brodsky have an easier time convincing us, since they defend poetry with such passion—and at times such captivating arrogance—that with any luck they put their opponent on the defensive. (Unfortunately, the opponent ordinarily doesn't even know that he's on the ropes; defenses of poetry are read, of course, only by its friends.)

Fortunately, we don't know precisely what poetry is, and we shouldn't try to figure it out analytically. No single definition (and there are so many) can finalize this element. And I, too, have no definitive ambitions. But there's something tempting, nonetheless, about seeing poetry in its movement "between"— both as one of the most important vehicles bearing us upward and as a way of understanding that ardor precedes irony. Ardor: the earth's fervent song, which we answer with our own, imperfect song.

We need poetry just as we need beauty (although I hear there are European countries in which this last word is strictly forbidden). Beauty isn't only for aesthetes; beauty is for anyone who seeks a serious road. It is a summons, a promise, if not of happiness, as Stendhal hoped, then of a great and endless journey.

"We truly must have commited a crime that brought down curses upon us, since we've lost the whole poetry of the cosmos." We've not only lost the poetry of the cosmos (and we lose it a little more every day, which proves, logically speaking, that we still haven't lost it completely, that we've been living for some time in something like a permanent state of losing, just as some governments thrive while continuously increasing their foreign debt). We've also experienced that peculiar bifurcation of sensibility that Thomas Mann depicts so precisely in his *Magic Mountain*. The poetry of the cosmos has divided—just like a cell observed by a modern scientist, a specialist in molecular biology—into Naphta's demonic whisper and the humanitarian discourse of Settembrini.

Thomas Mann did not invent this schism; it was rather a scrupulously observed diagnosis.

This is the misfortune of our times: that those who never make mistakes are mistaken, while those who make mistakes are right. Ernst Jünger in some of his observations concerning "substance," T. S. Eliot in parts of *Notes Towards the Definition of Culture*, and so many other conservative authors may not be wrong "ontologically" in their analyses of man in modernity. But they're completely immersed in the element of twentieth-century history and are blind to the phenomenal (and fragile) benefits we derive from liberal democracy. On the other hand, those who analyze our political troubles with exceptional acumen and respond to injustice are often completely at sea spiritually. Perhaps this is linked to Charles Taylor's brilliant observation in *Sources of the Self*: in our age, Enlightenment values have triumphed in public institutions, at least in the West, whereas in our private lives we abandon ourselves to Romantic insatiability. We go along with rationalism whenever public, social issues are at stake, but at home, in private, we search ceaselessly for the absolute and aren't content with the decisions we accept in the public sphere.

The antimetaphysical but politically dependable liberal left (or perhaps rather "center") and the potentially menacing but spiritually engaged right: one might summarize our peculiar bifurcation like this.

Since isn't it true that we're still dealing with the heroes of *The Magic Mountain*? With the exceptionally appealing Settembrini, who makes guest appearances on our television newscasts or runs a regular column in a popular newspaper where he defends democracy and humanistic values? We listen to him with interest, read his articles, but sometimes suspect him of a certain superficiality. And the demonic Naphta, whom we don't particularly like, doesn't he startle us at times with his exceptional insights into the world of culture? It's difficult to find Naphta on the television; he publishes his opinions in one of those obscure journals of which the happy majority of ordinary mortals has never heard.

When parliamentary elections draw near, we instinctively lean toward Settembrini, since we sense that for all his dishevelment he'll be able to direct us toward a suitable party, which may not save us (but elections aren't about salvation!) but also won't lead us astray, he won't guide us toward the abyss, toward some wretched, extreme political denouement.

However, once the electoral fever abates, when the respectable landscape of contemporary civilization is reinstated, doesn't Settembrini bore us just a bit, don't we begin to miss that interesting Mr. Naphta? Don't we long to chat with Naphta about our metaphysical anxieties (after all, he's an expert)? Won't he fascinate us with his notions about the world's fundamental unity? We'll forgive his dubious sense of humor, his awkwardness, if only he'll summon up that strange, sharp metaphysical shiver we require from time to time, which our amiable, honest Settembrini is unable to provide.

Another example: in an anthology of German essays edited by Ludwig Rohner many years ago, I stumbled upon a sketch by Ludwig Curtius (not to be confused with E. R. Curtius, the wonderful critic and literary historian) called "A Meeting in the Presence of Apollo Belvedere" ("*Begegnung beim Apollo von Belvedere*") from 1947. In the essay, Ludwig Curtius tells about his meeting (whether real or imagined) with a young German architect, a veteran who'd miraculously escaped the slaughter of the world war—as a soldier he'd been conscripted into the Wehrmacht and sent to fight on various fronts. This architect, worn by the horror of recent events, spends three evenings with the essay's author and gives three extraordinary lectures. The point of departure is the Apollo Belvedere, which had once been admired by Winckelmann and Goethe but had later been revealed to be, like so many other sculptures, a mere Roman copy, and whose reputation had thus suffered in the eyes of many professional art historians. The young architect nonetheless remains true to the Apollo Belvedere and sees in it a rare quality, which he calls "dignity" and finds lacking in many contemporary works of art. The next day he talks about the significance of "proportion" in the evaluation, and even more important, the experiencing of works of architecture. And finally, on the third day, he speaks passionately about the "mystery" present in great artworks, hidden within them like an apple's core.

The lectures we hear in the abbreviated form given by Ludwig Curtius are very beautiful.

The fourth day this brilliant, serious architect leaves—he sails to Argentina. For good. And thus the reader isn't sure if he isn't perhaps dealing with a figure more allegorical than actual. Since the whole essay might be read as a farewell to the metaphysical element in German culture. The essay's author, much older and more experienced, is dazzled by his young colleague and says farewell through him to the symbolic future of the German intelligentsia.

At the same time we hope that—if the young architect isn't made of allegorical matter—he's not someone who has serious reasons for wanting to hide from the postwar Allied tribunals in Argentina. (All of this, remember, takes place in Rome, which, as we know, didn't have the best reputation in the years immediately following the war.)

This last doubt is symptomatic—but also well-nigh automatic. Ardor, metaphysical seriousness, the risky voicing of strong opinions are all suspicious nowadays. They take the defendant's bench immediately, there's no need for lengthy, conscientious investigations. I have to confess, though, that in this case suspicions about the young architect's wartime history had occurred to me too.

The more general question comes out rather differently, though. This bifurcation of the spirit, this shifting of signs, this ongoing division between Settembrini, who loves the Enlightenment, and Naphta, who prefers the Middle Ages (or Romanticism), this split that means everyone who experiences powerful religious yearnings is almost automatically suspected of being a "right-winger"—is it simply a given? Or is this contemporary affliction curable?

After all, not every modern writer accommodates the laws of this bifurcation. Simone Weil would certainly have nothing to fear from an exam on the binary categories of *The Magic Mountain*. Or take Czeslaw Milosz's work, as rich intellectually as it is poetically. One of the hallmarks of this work is precisely its disregard for the arithmetic of easy ideological classifications. Milosz is, after all, the author of *The Land of Ulro*, among other things, an essay whose title is taken from Blake's private mythology. The book accuses our age of total indifference to metaphysical issues; it sorrowfully traces the slow decay of the religious imagination. Yet Milosz could hardly be called a "reactionary" writer, a disciple of Naphta. He's also, of course, the author of *The Captive Mind*, which is still fervently studied in all those countries where the intelligentsia can only dream of a rule of law (I've heard that Cuban intellectuals have been reading it recently). Milosz wrote both *The Land of Ulro* and *The Captive Mind*; careful readers of those very different books would surely never find a common language, they belong to two intellectual parties that aren't on speaking terms. But Milosz nonetheless manages to reconcile his concern with liberal civilization (which has expressed itself more than once in public forums) with powerful metaphysical yearnings.

Let's listen:

I keep my eyes closed. Do not rush me,
You, fire, power, might, for it is too early.
I have lived through many years and, as in this half-dream,
I felt I was attaining the moving frontier
Beyond which color and sound come true

And the things of this earth are united.
Do not yet force me to open my lips.
Let me trust and believe I will attain.
Let me linger here in Mittelbergheim.

I know I should. They are with me,
Autumn and wooden wheels and tobacco hung
Under the eaves. Here and everywhere
Is my homeland, wherever I turn
And in whatever language I would hear
The song of a child, the conversation of lovers.
Happier than anyone, I am to receive
A glance, a smile, a star, silk creased
At the knee. Serene, beholding,
I am to walk on hills in the soft glow of day
Over waters, cities, roads, human customs.

Fire, power, might, you who hold me
In the palm of your hand whose furrows
Are like immense gorges combed
By southern wind. You who grant certainty
In the hour of fear, in the week of doubt,
It is too early, let the wine mature,
Let the travelers sleep in Mittelbergheim.

(translated by Czeslaw Milosz and Richard Lourie)

This is an excerpt from the poem "Mittelbergheim," which
Milosz wrote in 1951, at a time—as we know from his own
commentary—when he was tormented by the ideological and political problems of the mid-twentieth century. He'd come under
ruthless attack by the émigré community when, after serving in
the communist diplomatic service for several years, he'd "chosen

freedom." These attacks drove him to despair, led him to doubt poetry. Alsatian Mittelbergheim, the village, or town, to which his friends had invited him—by happy onomastic coincidence, the place's name holds "mountain" as well as "middle" and "home"—offered him the possibility of inner rebirth. He had a spiritual experience, an experience of "something else," something one would be hard pressed to come upon in Paris, an enormous city as saturated with ideology, in the forties and fifties especially, as a sponge is with water and soapsuds; an experience of nature, world, fire.

The Alsatian town revealed to the poet a dimension transcending the ideological quarrels typical of the mid-twentieth century. The Alsatian town or perhaps simply the world, both archaic and contemporary, the world of mountains, vineyards, and the thick old walls of village homesteads.

Throughout Milosz's work, and not simply in this poem, we find a ceaseless wandering between ideas and transcendence, between the need for honesty and transparency in collective life, the need for the good, and, on the other hand, the unquenchable yearning for something more, for epiphany, for ecstasy, in which a higher sense is revealed (but never fully, and never completely clearly). Milosz's exceptional ability to withstand great pressures, his ability to move from social territory to the domain of metaphysics, endowed him with enormous poetic energy, an energy rarely encountered today. It derives from his ability to transform the condition of *metaxu* into an ongoing, vivifying pilgrimage, an occupation for the long-distance artist.

Nietzsche's followers will readily recall the myth of Anteus, who renews his strength only when he touches the earth. In his poetry Milosz has revised this myth, giving us an Anteus who recovers his strength by contact with both the earth and the sky.

The happily double-edged nature of Milosz's poetic (and essayistic) talent, his scrupulous attention to the truth of collective life and a higher, ecstatic truth, has enabled him to create a body of work before which both Naphta and Settembrini must stop short—not only with profound respect but with great interest. Perhaps, then, true ardor doesn't divide; it unifies. And it leads neither to fanaticism nor to fundamentalism. Perhaps one day ardor will return to our bookstores, our intellects.

2 The Shabby and the Sublime

Il n'est pas de poésie sans hauteur . . .
—Philippe Jaccottet

Whenever we speak of anything more general than, say, the view from our own window (a cherry branch, and behind it the late afternoon's cloudy sky), we risk being charged with arbitrariness. You might say it that way, but then again—the critic scoffs—it could be put quite differently. Pandemonium prevails in the realm of general propositions, something like the chaos of a barracks abandoned an hour earlier by a regiment out for spring training.

I'm touchy about this particular accusation: poets are especially sensitive to the charge of arbitrariness. Poetry, after all, involves precision and concreteness; words are verified not, as Rudolf Carnap would have it, through empirical, quantifiable observations. They are verified through existential preparedness, through experience, through our own lives, through reflection and moments of illumination. But they *are* verified. They don't appear randomly. Only provincial physics teachers who down a few beers every night could conceive of poetry as the realm of absolute license.

But when someone who works alone in the concrete domain of poetry ventures into the realm of general propositions—like a carpenter who's been asked to talk on the problems of European forest administration—he must shield his brow, take a deep breath, and with quick, unflinching steps traverse this treacherous terrain. And so to me, writing and thinking in recent years have come to seem meager, gray, anemic. More specifically, the output of recent years—I'll take poetry as my example, since that's what I follow most closely—is marked by a disproportion between the high style and the low, between powerful expressions of the inner life and the ceaseless chatter of self-satisfied craftsmen. I have the sense that we're up against a kind of fainthearted appeasement, a policy of evasions and concessions as concerns the literary vocation. And I see one of the chief symptoms of this weakness in the decline of high style and the overwhelming predominance of a low style, tepid, ironic, conversational.

Let me state from the start that I don't speak as a conservative. I don't recommend a return to medieval Christianity, the Renaissance, or even something as close at hand as European Romanticism. And I won't bemoan the dearth of talent, since I don't see any dearth of gifted writers. I want only to describe the situation as I see it, running the risk at every moment of committing some faux pas, of alienating socialists or sportsmen, stamp collectors or supporters of education and hygienic housing. I won't propose a diagnosis; you diagnose when you're young and ambitious, but the time comes later for meditation and, at most, the distress sometimes accompanied by something like a chuckle.

How did this all get started? Do we know?

At times we may unexpectedly catch sight of how things used to be before the mutation of European literature. In Robert Graves's remarkable memoir *Goodbye to All That*, we find the following description of a meeting with Siegfried Sassoon:

> Siegfried Sassoon had, at the time, published only a few privately-printed pastoral pieces of eighteen-ninetyish flavor . . . We went to the cake shop and ate cream buns. At this time I was getting my first book of poems, *Over the Brazier*, ready for the press; I had one or two drafts in my pocket-book and showed them to Siegfried. He frowned and said that war should not be written about in such a realistic way. In return, he showed me some of his own poems. One of them began:
>
> > *Return to greet me, colours that were my joy,*
> > *Not in the woeful crimson of men slain . . .*
>
> Siegfried had not yet been in the trenches. I told him, in my old soldier manner, that he would soon change his style.

The trenches of the First World War led to what was probably an inevitable change of style. They thrust writers in the direction of an outraged realism. Did they also lead to a gradual evolution of human nature? Graves's generation had a quarrel with the silver-tongued orators of the Victorian era, with impassioned elocutionists, abusers of high-flown speech such as d'Annunzio in Italy. The splendid Eugenio Montale constructed his poetics precisely against the grandiloquence of poets like d'Annunzio. Above all the poets of Graves's generation despised the hysterical style of journalists and generals. After his return to England from the front, Graves recalls, it was months before he could bear the publicists' patriotic syntax. Disgustedly he quotes a letter written by a "little mother" intended to persuade other British mothers that they should rejoice in their sons' valiant deaths! Having experienced the horror of war, the rats in the trenches, the campaigns to "no man's land" where unburied German and English corpses lay rotting, Graves was now confronted, and revolted, by the pronouncements of British chauvinism. During a war, generals—and their wives—employ the high style. It enters naturally into the service of propaganda.

In the trenches of the First World War, and more unimaginably, the camps of the Second World War, people saw things no one should see, things that, in calmer times, would be experienced only by a few unfortunates standing eye to eye with their own murderers. It is probably impossible to create an art that could answer to the terror of those extreme experiences in a trustworthy and consistent way, that would "scale the heights" of the lowest depths in modern history. These radical experiences inevitably lead in the end to a rejection of Mozart's sonatas and Keats's odes. Someone will always turn up to insist that literature is just literature and music is only music; and that person, as harrowed as Job (or perhaps just a precocious student at a prestigious university), will be right. It is just literature, it is only music. That's the best we have.

The young Tadeusz Rozewicz, a poet who came not from the camps but from the forests that generously hid the partisans of World War II, effected something like an about-face in Polish poetry. He stripped it of its complex syntax, its velvety similes, and baroque accumulation of tropes, and replaced them with a radical starkness of expression.

To be sure, this simplification of style, which was often strikingly successful and opened new vistas in art, was brought about by a multitude of factors. The pressure of modernity made itself felt in all forms of art, not just in poetry. The onslaught of social criticism, descended from the Enlightenment and coupled with what Ortega y Gasset called "the revolt of the masses," joined forces with the disillusionment of the Romantic poet who had failed to persuade the masses to his vision (the French literary historian Paul Benichou dissects this phenomenon beautifully) and imbued poetry with its sardonic humor. Louis MacNeice once remarked that Auden managed to "put the soul across in telegrams." Auden and a few others were able to pull this off, but there was no shortage of poets who were almost fatally paralyzed by these stark means of expression; their souls became telegraph forms.

The trouble is that great simplicity—and everyone who seeks both beauty and truth has dreamt of it—achieves its bracing effect only by contrast with complex, baroque forms, and the result is never lasting. The moment of transformation, the instant of contrast, passes quickly. It's like a surgical procedure which is not supposed to last long—unless you forget about the patient. Tadeusz Rozewicz remains an outstanding poet, but today he achieves more rarely the almost supernatural simplicity of his early poetry.

Paradoxically, the purging of aesthetics under the influence of horror, the simplification of art by shock, leads in the long run to an aesthetics that can express neither horror nor shock. (It's worth noting that neither Milosz, who survived the Nazi terror, nor Mandelstam, who didn't survive the Stalinist nightmare, ever fell prey to the lure of a false simplicity.)

I'll give another example. My friend Tzvetan Todorov, with

whom I often agree and occasionally argue, published an essay several years ago called "Eloge du quotidien," or "In Praise of the Quotidian," a discussion of several paintings from the golden age of Dutch painting. Todorov rightly admires the Dutch masters, about whom we may say (following Neruda, as cited by Seamus Heaney) that thanks to them "the world's reality will not go unremarked." Here is the world's reality, in this poetry of dim interiors, in these still lifes, *natures mortes*, disclosing the delicate being of things, paintings in which onions and leeks achieve the dignity of royal silk, portraits of men and women who were neither kings nor princes, but who merited nonetheless a depiction full of tenderness. How can we comprehend the sensitivity of these painters, we who regularly fear that reality will melt beneath our fingers, for whom even the movies, unlike the vibrating electrons of television, seem somehow pleasantly old-fashioned, since they can at least occasionally convey people and objects in their absolute, opaque presence.

But the aims of Todorov's elegant essay extend beyond the philosophical treatment of art history. The essay serves a normative, programmatic purpose. It attempts to establish a sphere of life—and a corresponding sphere of art—from which certain elements are excluded. "In Praise of the Quotidian" presents a program for life and art, an antimetaphysical program. It confers special ontological status upon the quotidian. We must adore the quotidian, value it, so as not to seek refuge in nostalgia, utopias, or fantasies. It summons us to live in the present moment, to root ourselves in reality. But at what cost? Here is Todorov:

> The genre painter is not satisfied only to renounce history; he makes a choice, and a highly restrictive choice, among all the actions that make up the tissue of human

life. He renounces the representation of everything that exceeds the ordinary, and remains inaccessible to the majority of mortals. There is no place here for heroes and saints. When Karel Capek visited Holland, he remarked that the Dutch painters must have done their painting sitting down . . .

I resist precisely this pruning, this reduction of reality, this contraction of human life—and art!—to a narrow zone that holds no place for heroes and saints. It's not that I want to propagate heroics or compose hagiographies; I have something else in mind. On the level of aesthetics, contact with the sublime gives us the equivalent of "heroes" and "saints." This contact is never unadulterated—we have such thick skin these days that we probably couldn't stand an epic poem that functioned only as a conduit to the sublime, that didn't amuse and puzzle us at the same time. Still it remains indispensable for art. How little divides us finally from Longinus and his classic work on the sublime, written in the early years of our era. The literary encyclopedia reminds us that the sublime is not a formal feature of a work and can't be defined by way of rhetorical categories. It is instead "a spark that leaps from the soul of the writer to the soul of his reader." Has so much really changed? Don't we still wait greedily for that spark?

Surely we don't go to poetry for sarcasm or irony, for critical distance, learned dialectics or clever jokes. These worthy qualities and forms perform splendidly in their proper place—in an essay, a scholarly tract, a broadside in an opposition newspaper. In poetry, though, we seek the vision, the fire, the flame that accompanies spiritual revelation. In short, from poetry we expect poetry.

Todorov's gesture is dangerous—it rends the rich fabric of

reality, the cloth that we received whole from previous generations and that we are obliged to pass on undamaged to generations yet to come. It is a web of human experience holding room for heroism and saints, for madness, tragedy, and reason—as well as for laughter, of course, and the quotidian, since the quotidian, too, is beautiful. But it is beautiful not least because we sense in it the quiet quivering of potential events, enigmatic, heroic, exceptional events. The quotidian is like the surface of a peaceful, low-lying river, where delicate currents and eddies are etched, auguring rushes and floods that may or may not come to pass. The mute lightning bolts in the sky don't trouble us for now, they are omens of distant storms. But those storms will reach us one day. A notion of the quotidian that omits all possibility of heroism and saintliness—the shiver of a tragedy still distant—is flat and monotonous. Moreover, it is not true to life, and hence cannot form the ontological basis for a persuasive aesthetics. I am not in thrall, I hope, to what the Polish critic Karol Irzykowski called "the highbrow mania for tragedy"; but I insist that a complete sundering of the sublime must finally lead to a world of chess-playing computers, not living, mortal, humans.

Todorov concludes one section of his essay with a description of a painting by Pieter de Hooch called *Mother and Children*, which hangs in Berlin. In the picture's background we see a girl gazing at the world. "The girl is not looking at anything," Todorov writes, "she turns her eyes toward the emptiness outside, smitten by a spell that has stolen her away from the real world. The whole of life, the infinity of the universe, drives her on. She regards the light."

In this passage, one of my favorites, we glimpse a way to revise Todorov's narrow program, although it remains unrealized.

Precisely because the world that opens before the chubby little girl is boundless and mysterious—the painting just hints at "the world" as the northern daylight invades the cozy bourgeois interior through a half-open door—it must encompass both the known and the unknown. Neither heroism nor saintliness can be axiomatically excluded, any more than one can remove the ultraviolet rays from daylight or expel the dead from the earth. But Todorov wants precisely this; he wants to purify the earth, to diminish it.

"In Praise of the Quotidian" is a brilliant work; on first reading, it completely won me over. It is marked, though, by a kind of *trahison des clercs*, a breach of faith. It betrays a strong—too strong?—affinity with the mood of our unheroic era. But it is surely a clerk's duty to open himself to the world beyond clerkdom. He must think and judge without yielding to the temper of the times. "Philosophy is the epoch's judge, but things go ill when it becomes the epoch's mouthpiece," Rudolf Pannwitz observes, as Hofmannsthal reports in his astonishing *Book of Friends*.

The sublime must be understood differently these days, of course. The concept must be stripped of its neoclassical pomp, its alpine stage set, its theatrical overkill. The sublime today is chiefly a perception of the world's mysteries, a metaphysical shudder, an astonishment, an illumination, a sense of proximity to what cannot be put into words. (It goes without saying that these shudders must take a persuasive artistic form.)

I mentioned madness among the elements that make up that great reality of which we are the trustees, thanks to the very significant accident of our birth. The marvelous little-known Italian essayist Nicola Chiaromonte—a political émigré, antifascist, and friend of André Malraux and Albert Camus, he died in Rome in January 1972—wrote in an essay on Shakespeare:

But in the world today madness has been eliminated for reasons of dogma: in our world only the most rigorous rationalism is given voice, and thus absurdity erupts on every front, and the claims of human madness, which insists on its due share, turn into bitter rebellion and a passion for destruction.

Our great reality obviously contains many other elements as well. Can we count them all? Should we?

They include not only darkness, tragedy, and madness but also joy. Not long ago I was rereading the essays of Jerzy Stempowski, a major Polish essayist who spent the second half of his life as a humble émigré in Switzerland, in Berne, where he died in 1969. And I came upon a surprising quotation from Maupassant—surprising, since you don't expect metaphysical gifts from naturalists! I must have come across it earlier, but its force struck me this time.

From time to time I experience strange, intense, short-lived visions of beauty, an unfamiliar, elusive, barely perceptible beauty that surfaces in certain words or landscapes, certain colorations of the world, certain moments . . . I'm not able to describe or communicate it, I can't express it or portray it. I save these moments for myself . . . I have no other reason for continuing, no other cause for keeping on . . .

"Strange, intense, short-lived visions of beauty"—how could we live without them! "I can't describe it," Maupassant says. And we discover in his account something very familiar that is also very difficult to convey. In such moments one experiences something incomprehensible and piercing, both extravagant and absolutely fundamental.

Origen thought that those who have been fully initiated into a religion's substance come to live in a spirit of eternal joy, an unending holiday. Only novices, he said, require the labored cheerleading of official church holidays! It is very clear that we who live today are not among the initiates; our holidays last only moments.

And these ephemeral revelations of beauty are coupled in some strange way with moments of great sorrow, of overwhelming grief. Yet neither one nor the other is simply a personal whim, a mere mood swing; both the joy and the sorrow correspond to something in reality itself. We don't exactly know what causes beauty; suffering's causes are easier to guess.

This mixture of impermanence and permanence, the blending of what vanishes and what remains, is yet another ingredient of our reality—that is, if we choose not to be reductionists. A workman's shovel may suddenly uncover a pocket mirror of gold flashing among the ordinary, rough, unpolished lodes. Mortal and immortal moments likewise mingle in the abundance of our everyday existence. I suppose there are far more of the former than the latter, but who knows? Has anyone counted?

I don't want to enlist in the ranks of those poets who praise poetry so passionately as to negate the worth of every other form of communication. The great, lamented Joseph Brodsky even said that anyone who follows traffic laws has clearly read poetry beforehand; aesthetics preceded ethics for Brodsky. But when I watch classic films—my wife and I just watched Marcel Carné's legendary film *Quai des brumes* (1938), which Vichy propaganda accused of demoralizing France and thus leading to the defeat of 1940!—I feel moved and bored simultaneously. Film ages far more quickly than the other arts. The "world's eye" of any given time reaches its apogee in film. The styles of watching, walking, and filming, the camera angles, the fashions (clothes, makeup, smiles, gestures, anger, and affection): all these tiny "contemporaneities" change every eight or ten years. Unlike the realist novel, poetry largely ignores them, but they take up permanent residence in films, which fade like aging photographs. Poetry is among the arts that fade the least.

I know that such ideas may seem laughable. Hollywood releases new films every minute, new *Titanics*, which, unlike the original, navigate screen seas successfully, garnering billions of dollars in the process. We hear nothing (or even less than nothing) about poets, though, and one of these nonentities dares to doubt the durability of the dream factory's productions!

A poet—less than nothing! In his essay "Der Dichter und seine Zeit," Hugo von Hofmannsthal compares the poet to the medieval saint Alexis, and the comparison only grows apter with time.

> Does he not resemble that princely pilgrim of the old legend, who was commanded to abandon his princely home and wife and family and set out for the Holy Land; he returned thence, but before he crossed the threshold he was bidden to enter his own home disguised as a beggar known to no one, and he took up his abode where the servants ruled. The servants ordered him to take his place beneath the stairs, where the dogs were kept at night. And there he lives and sees his wife, brothers and children as they climb and descend the stairs, and he hears how they speak of him as lost or even dead and he thus discovers how they mourn for him. But he has been commanded not to let himself

be known, and so he lives on unrecognized in his very
home . . . For thus it is given that the master of the
house shall not master his own possessions—for does
the master of the house possess the dark that fills his
halls at night, does he possess the cook's insolence, the
stable boy's conceit, the sighing of the meekest serving
girl? But he who dwells in darkness like a spirit shall
own all!

I don't know if the Polish poet Kazimiera Illakowiczowna
was responding to Hofmannsthal's essay when she wrote a poem
in which St. Alexis's unhappy wife bemoans God's stern sentence; she is, after all, the victim of this pious experiment.
Unlike her husband, who basks in reality's shadow, she owns
neither day nor night, neither drawing rooms nor dusky halls.
Her lot is sorrow and distress; and her monologue is a lament for
a wasted life. I'd like to hear the same kind of lament issuing
from the modern world, a world divorced from poetry and given
over to the Internet and ads.

When we open the paper, though, we generally find a splendid catalogue of temporary things (unless it's an unusually historic day: the liberation of Paris, the fall of the Berlin Wall, the
death of Napoleon). If we read very carefully, we may be able
to recall the name of the UN secretary-general. Such things
change quickly. The Politburo of a certain totalitarian party has
ceased to exist, and today's children will never know how sinister
the word itself once was, how people feared its "proceedings," its
"resolutions," its "censures." But where do we find what's lasting? Where do the deathless things hide?

With their chins high, girls come back from the tennis courts.
The spray rainbows over the sloping lawns.

With short jerks a robin runs up, stands motionless.
The eucalyptus tree trunks glow in the light.
The oaks perfect the shadow of May leaves.
Only this. Only this is worthy of praise: the day.

(Czeslaw Milosz, from "Throughout Our Lands")

Imperishable things drift through the air, mixed with what is passing; it's someone's job to sort them out.

But can we still write like Hölderlin, like Norwid, like Yeats, like Rilke, like Mandelstam, like Milosz, in a way that directs us to the world's wholeness, to a world that holds divinity and pain, joy and despair—and not like a professional who's mastered one subject perfectly and is interested in only one thing, be it language, politics, or acacia blossoms? Must we become deft miniaturists with a single theme? And what should the high style be today? Almost certainly not hieratic utterances, in the manner of Claudel or Saint-John Perse. They are wonderful poets, but they lack a sense of humor; and a high style unaccompanied by a sense of humor—a sense of humor brimming with forbearance for our cruel, comic, and imperfect world—would become a chilly mausoleum. It would be like those quarries outside Tuscan Carrara from which the marble has been stripped, leaving only whiteness.

The high style grows from a ceaseless dialogue between two spheres, the spiritual realm whose guardians and creators are the dead (like Virgil in the *Divine Comedy*) and the domain of eternal *praesens*, our single, precious moment, the pocket of time in which we've chanced to live. The high style mediates between the spirits of the past and the stopgaps of the present; between Virgil and the young people wearing Walkmen as they rollerblade along Western Europe's slick sidewalks; between poor, lonely Hölderlin and tipsy German tourists whooping it up along the narrow streets of Lucca; between the vertical and the horizontal.

But the problem is that the high style is not really a "middle-man" by nature, like Hermes in ancient Greece or Thomas Mann in the twentieth century. The high style arises in response to final things. It is a reaction to mystery, to what is loftiest. But how does one mediate between what is high and what is flat? Surely the outcome of such a negotiation can only be a mathematical mean, a kind of measured leveling, a relative drop on the spirit's stock market. No, this "mediation" must be very subtle. There can be no talk of simply seeking some happy mean between the great and small. The rigorous mediation I have in mind involves instead a certain discomfort with contemporary society; it deals with placement, incarnation; it requires the humor and the irony, painful at times, that keep one from slipping into scorn. The contemporary writer has his feet caught in the rather absurd and comfortable little world of consumer society. And not just his feet; he is stuck in this world up to his knees, even his waist. He's been infected by the comic passions on which this little world thrives.

At the same time, though, thanks not only to his reading but to his moments of solitude, and to experiences of the kind that Freud (I should at least mention him once) called "oceanic," the writer occasionally gains access to more serious realms of being. So perhaps the high style is not about mediation so much as about a certain kind of metaphysical modesty, about humor (*anch'io sono consumatore*), about learning to open up to the beautiful, the sublime. Nothing reactionary or ridiculous is required to achieve this; you don't need to drape yourself in ancient tunics like Stefan George and his circle of acolytes, who, engulfed by the vulgarity of Wilhelmine Germany, performed Hellenic plays on the rooftops of apartment buildings.

Humor is crucial for the high style, since we must also understand that we will never completely succeed in tidying the world, even if the high style typically aspires to a highly ordered reality. We continue to desire the high style, we continue to require its presence—but we can no longer believe wholeheartedly that we'll complete our exhaustive inventory of the cosmos.

Strong in reading, thought, and experience, but weak in practice; mired in modernity like Seamus Heaney's mummies dredged up from ancient bogs; weak, too, like all modern men, in the mentality exposed by the theorists, the mentality of a "man without qualities": the writer in search of "high style" does not cease to be an "everyman." He is weak like everyone else; like everyone else he falls prey to the temptations of mindless television and American movies. He knows full well the dreariness of highways and vacationing crowds. He is stronger perhaps only in his unflagging drive to seek out something higher, in his recollection of the sublime, which he refuses to write off as modernity's loss (as his fellow travelers and beachside companions might see it).

Anyway, we're not in danger of creating a high style that would arise chiefly or exclusively from a distaste for modernity. Precisely such a distaste for modernity defined the rhetorical choices of the great and less great writers in our not-so-distant past. This misadventure befell the generation of our grandfathers (Ernst Jünger, Pierre Drieu La Rochelle, André Malraux, Ernest Hemingway, Gottfried Benn, Vladimir Mayakovsky, Henry de Montherlant, Bertolt Brecht; with Yeats and T. S. Eliot in the place of honor). A generation of "violent writers" was repelled by the torpid, horizontal world of modern democracy, by a modern society governed not by kingly flourishes but by the shocks of the stock market and the tallies of parliament. They performed and promoted bold action, valiant deeds. They were knights, worshippers of corrida, warriors, noblemen, seducers, revolutionaries, nationalists, commissars. The deed—military, erotic, or aristocratic—was a metaphor, a pretext for high style, a rhetoric of ardent action whose goal was to throw off the modern world and recast it in a nobler alloy (though no one knew precisely what this better metal should be); it made no difference whether this better substance was forged on the left or the right, so long as it was radical. Recent European memory has been imprinted with the notion that high style must always be an instrument of reaction, a hammer smashed against modernity.

It is a misguided notion. We who as children played gleefully and from necessity among the ruins we inherited through the deeds of our valiant, eloquent forebears—not writers, needless to say, who, when they awakened from their youthful madness, rarely poked their heads from their vast studies—we're skeptical of that rhetoric, that version of high style, that knowing air. We also realize that modernity can't be fought (you won't win), even if it needs chiding upon occasion, even if one of its less intelligent faces repels us. Modernity must be improved, expanded, enhanced, enriched; we must speak to it. Modernity resides within us; it's too late to attack it from the sidelines.

I've often wondered whether the marked composure of the present generation of writers, writers who no longer want to be knights or bold officers whose faces, etched in scars, draw soldiers into battle, or ruthless revolutionaries with exotic noms de guerre, stems from a deliberate choice, from the conscious acceptance of an inner sensitivity, or whether it is also a predictable reaction to a tiring excess of noisy rhetoric, a simple desire for change. To put it differently, do we prefer Vermeer to Rubens because we've carefully compared the value of contemplation to the value of (dubious) radical action? Or are we governed simply by fashion, public sentiment, by what other people think? Does wisdom guide us, or mere conformism? This last possibility would force us to take a pessimistic view of literature's future (and other futures as well).

Several years ago the French minister of foreign affairs ironically chastised the French intellectuals who had violently attacked the sluggish European policy in Bosnia for not actually going to Bosnia to fight the aggressor as Malraux, Simone Weil, and so many others had done during the Spanish Civil War. He failed to consider the change of generations, the altered attitudes. Those who cherish the dialogical principle and the murmur of laptop computers are not likely to take up arms on the battlefield. For that you need a generation of adventurers like our grandfathers.

High style need no longer stem from a dislike of modernity. But low style—ironic, colloquial, flat, small, minimal—may arise precisely from *ressentiment*, from a rejection of our silver-tongued forebears. Perhaps not everywhere, in all linguistic spheres. Certainly those who read German may have received the impression more than once that there exists to this day a prohibition on "sublimity" and "metaphysics" in German literature, as if everything higher, bolder, unironically intellectual must be linked by necessity to a pernicious past, thus leading— yes!—onto politically treacherous, fascist territory.

Thus the contemporary writer stumbles upon a problem basic to any artistic creation. Do we concede, in democracy's exceedingly sober spirit, that we make our pronouncements in an empty room, that we draw exclusively upon ourselves, our own spiritual lives, our own mentality, as we confess our venal sins and minor revelations; or, as antiquity and the Middle Ages believed, and as the Romantics still hoped, subject to the more or less visible authority of a truth residing somewhere outside our own skulls?

It's a difficult question. No one would want to relinquish the freedom we achieved through the European revolts against churchly authority. In acknowledging the invisible authority of a truth beyond ourselves, wouldn't we inevitably be squandering three hundred years of hard-won European emancipation, the emancipation of citizens, of individuals, of men and women? Anyway, we can neither discard the Enlightenment nor erase it from our history. I've already mentioned the essayist Jerzy Stempowski. In his book *Terre bernoise* he writes about the trees of central Switzerland. He comments in the eighteenth century, linden trees, which are consecrated to love and Venus, began to be planted at the spot where the local gallows had stood (on the outskirts, the *Galgenberg*) in virtually every village. Anyone who has longed in a fit of rage to expunge the Enlightenment from our past would do well to remember the lindens, those lovely trees with the intoxicating scent (it's no accident that they were linked to Venus), that took the place of the gallows' dry wood so recently—not much over two hundred years ago. The trees would almost certainly not be here today if it weren't for the fussy eighteenth century and its wigs.

There can be no question of a "return" to some rigorously ordered "medieval" transcendence. Eliot's late directives advising poets to subject themselves to an impersonal discipline and to enroll in the ranks of a higher spiritual order, the order of *caritas*, seem pedantic: they reek of the church vestibule. And yet the intuition of which artists often speak, the power that permits an artist to formulate a poem's most pointed words or a sonata's most crucial notes, still deserves our best attention. Maybe we're not altogether alone in our empty room, in our workshop: if so many writers love solitude it may be because they're not really all that lonely. There really is a higher voice that sometimes—too rarely—speaks. We catch it only in the moments of our greatest concentration. This voice may only speak once, it may make itself heard only after long years of waiting: still, it changes everything. For it means that the freedom we cherish, the freedom we seek, is not our only treasure. The voice we sometimes hear does not deprive us of our liberty; it demonstrates only that this freedom has its limits, that emancipation can take us only so far.

For this reason, I'm stubbornly prepared to defend the notion of "inspiration," the notion Paul Valéry, that great professor of poetry, treated so contemptuously. Inspiration doesn't absolve anyone from exacting labor and strict discipline; but inspiration —which differs for every artist and assumes new guises every time, guises unified only by the Muse's familiar form—is what guides us toward that voice. (The Muse survives today only in humorous forms, but she once provoked complex emotions. Robert Graves notes that the Muse aroused feelings ranging from ecstasy to revulsion, powerfully religious feelings.) Inspiration is short-lived, of course—but its fleeting presence is important, it cleanses something in us, it opens us to that voice which we understand so poorly, but whose absence would leave us little wiser than any of the other mammals.

The English language has a very useful word, "cant," meaning humbug, high-flown lying, rhetoric. I think that everyone who speaks of high style today must bear in mind the countless rhetorical possibilities for its abuse, the new variants of cant that range from odes to Stalin and other tyrants to the thousands of wretched amateur verses singing the praises of flowers or naively lauding a naive God. We cannot escape retracing Bertolt Brecht's path, his class-based suspicion of Parnassian poetasting—but we can't rid ourselves of skepticism toward facile pathos so easily. Every era needs its own diction; anyone who praises high style by means of anachronistic, Symbolist syntax—or Victorian syntax in the Anglo-American context—courts ridicule. We've also learned to marvel at details, the concrete; high diction today must preserve this form of revelation and not seek refuge in lofty clichés.

A stirring passage from Aleksander Wat's memoirs comes to mind. The memoirs were taped as Wat told the story of his life to Czeslaw Milosz, and they were published many years after Wat's death under the title *My Age*. As a young poet, Wat was much taken with Dadaism: linguistic experimentation, a playful critique of language as such enthralled him. He speaks to Milosz about the change of heart he experienced in a Moscow prison, the Lubyanka (a prison from which very few emerged alive, and survivors were packed off to Siberia). There he understood that the language entrusted to a poet is extraordinarily precious and fragile, and in grave peril; and the poet's task is to nurture this language, not to mock it. This prison anecdote, so well known to Polish readers and critics, has symbolic significance. It points to a watershed between two currents in twentieth-century poetry; and it places this turning point on the map. Critics seldom mention these two currents; they're preoccupied with other, less obvious aesthetic phenomena. The first of these two trends is critical, avant-garde, analytic, and suspicious. The second, which draws far fewer followers, is more constructive than destructive, more ecstatic than sardonic. It seeks out what is hidden. The Lubyanka must have been the best possible place for such reflections.

Even if they were lucky enough to escape the Lubyanka, the poets of Central Europe knew full well about the existence of these two currents and they understood Wat's perception perfectly. Not all of them drew radical conclusions from Wat's change of heart. But one poet who would surely have agreed with Wat was Zbigniew Herbert.

One day Herbert showed up at our high school in Gliwice. Our high school was not exactly a hotbed of poetry, to put it mildly. All our time was taken up with parties, first dates, bike rides, Elvis Presley, Chubby Checker, and Little Richard, to say nothing of life itself, which we understood mainly as fairly shallow musings on a very distant future. If the school's more ambitious students (I will admit to being one of them) read anything more serious, our taste was dictated by current fashion. We read the theater of the absurd, which filled the "Notebook" section of the journal *Dialogue*. And we adored bleak writing: the pitiless Kafka, with his gaunt, malnourished face, was our god. Our own country's writers didn't especially interest us; we were snobs. (Small countries often rebuff their own writers.)

This young man was already a famous poet, even if he was better known among the Warsaw and Krakow cognoscenti than among us provincials. Meeting high school students at one in the afternoon must have been utter drudgery, a way to pick up the modest fee provided by the district superintendent. (He had probably lectured that morning at a school in Bytom, and was likely en route to a reading in Katowice later that evening.) But his visit changed my view of literature. Not right away; but slowly and steadily. I followed his work attentively from then on, and I noticed that, unlike certain absurdists, Herbert had no parti pris, no a priori theory of the world. In place of dogma, I found a flexible, unforced, search for meaning; flexible, like a person crossing an Italian town at dawn. His poetry was marked by the war, by the occupation, by the dingy totalitarianism of the Soviet state. But it retained a certain humanist buoyancy, a serenity.

Zbigniew Herbert died in July of 1998 at the age of seventy-three. It may still be too soon to seek his work's "defining formula." (Perhaps such formulas are best ignored in any case.) But he's important to my argument on "high style." He was a poet who never settled into a single stylistic costume. He opposed what he called "whimpering" (and this from the poet of a country that in modern history had known more defeats than victories!). As he wrote in his poem "Why the Classics":

> if art for its subject
> will have a broken jar
> a small broken soul
> with a great self-pity
>
> what will remain after us
> will be like lovers' weeping
> in a small dirty hotel
> when wall-paper dawns
>
> (translated by Czeslaw Milosz and Peter Dale Scott)

"The Envoy of Mr. Cogito" remains Herbert's great hymn. It is a poem in which skepticism joins hands with the sublime, in which the "clown's face" speaks great words:

Go where those others went to the dark boundary
for the golden fleece of nothingness your last prize

go upright among those who are on their knees
among those with their backs turned and those toppled in the
    dust

you were saved not in order to live
you have little time you must give testimony

be courageous when the mind deceives you be courageous
in the final account only this is important

and let your helpless Anger be like the sea
whenever you hear the voice of the insulted and beaten

let your sister Scorn not leave you
for the informers executioners cowards—they will win
they will go to your funeral and with relief will throw a lump of
    earth
the woodborer will write your smoothed-over biography

and do not forgive truly it is not in your power
to forgive in the name of those betrayed at dawn

beware however of unnecessary pride
keep looking at your clown's face in the mirror
repeat: I was called—weren't there better ones than I

beware of dryness of heart love the morning spring
the bird with an unknown name the winter oak

light on a wall the splendor of the sky
they don't need your warm breath
they are there to say: no one will console you

be vigilant—when the light on the mountain gives the sign—
     arise and go
as long as blood turns in the breast your dark star

repeat old incantations of humanity fables and legends
because this is how you will attain the good you will not attain
repeat great words repeat them stubbornly
like those crossing the desert who perished in the sand

and they will reward you with what they have at hand
with the whip of laughter with murder on a garbage heap

go because only in this way will you be admitted to the
     company of cold skulls
to the company of your ancestors: Gilgamesh Hector Roland
the defenders of the kingdom without limit and the city of
     ashes

Be faithful Go

                              (translated by John and Bogdana Carpenter)

We are so prosaic, so ordinary. Do we even deserve poetry? But
we, too, will be legends for future generations, because we once
lived, and our word will mean more than we care to admit today.

3 Nietzsche in Krakow

I discovered Nietzsche's writings during my student years. I scoured Krakow's used book stores for them when it was still relatively easy to come upon beautiful editions of Nietzsche's work from the early years of the century, as translated by first-rate Polish writers and poets under the imprint of "Jakob Mortkowicz, Publisher." You couldn't find Nietzsche in bookstores carrying current publications, though, since Nietzsche had been officially denounced—in all the so-called socialist realist countries, I suspect—as "a precursor of fascism." But who hadn't been denounced? Nietzsche found himself in good company. Czeslaw Milosz, George Orwell, Arthur Koestler, Hannah Arendt, Raymond Aron had all been condemned, along with many others. Whoever didn't like totalitarianism and came right out and said so ended up on the blacklist. To be fair—and here I hear the voice of some retired censor pointing out my error—Nietzsche was actually on a different list, where his neighbors were Celine, Goebbels, *Mein Kampf*, the works of the Italian fascist ideologists, and so on. That's all well and good, but the fact remains that he couldn't be found in normal bookstores, and all you had to do was read around in twentieth-century literature, whether poetry or prose, to come upon the tracks of a mysterious writer, different from the rest, belonging to a separate category—the tracks of a master who didn't write a single novel, a poet unlike "ordinary" poets, a writer who made the essay his chief weapon, an artist who died a lunatic after years of wandering through the countries of Southern Europe. The encyclopedias we had on hand said nothing. They explained in their lapidary, lying style that he was "a precursor of fascism who paved the way for bourgeois irrationalism," or something equally idiotic. But no one particularly trusted the encyclopedias put out by the communists, so you had to look elsewhere, seek out those fine old books published at the turn of the century. Sometimes you'd stumble on a photograph, always the same one, a man with a mustache and thick dark hair, very serious, intense, slightly affected.

Nietzsche was a mysterious figure to me and my contemporaries back in the seventies. We knew something about his unhappy love affair with the beautiful Russian Lou Andreas, about his illness, his alpine strolls, his ghastly migraines. But we couldn't be sure, we lacked particulars. Things must have been completely different in the West, of course, where there was no dearth of scholarly studies, biographies, bibliographies, where Nietzsche's place in the nineteenth-century tradition was debated, to be sure, but no one was in doubt about the basic facts. Eastern Europe's belatedness—caused by the war and the communist censorship, since there'd been no problem with studying or simply reading Nietzsche before—was in a certain sense a blessing, since it allowed us to experience the same shiver of emotion that his first readers must have felt, representatives of the first generation to fall under the author of *Zarathustra*'s spell. Nietzsche emerged from anonymity, after all, only in the closing years of the nineteenth century, and very little was known about him at first. By stripping Nietzsche of his right to literary existence, the communist censorship locked him up, after its own fashion, in a lunatic asylum and unwittingly restored the glory of the *poète maudit*.

Apart from the legend of the author, though, what struck me in Nietzsche's own texts? I began, I think, with *The Birth of Tragedy*, *Human*, *All-Too-Human*, and *The Dawn*—but the sequence in which I read them was dictated, I should add, by which books I managed to track down in the used book stores, and then in the larger libraries. By chance, though, it turned out to be more or less the order in which the books appeared. My first readings of Nietzsche endure in my memory as a festival of freedom; there was something liberating in their message. After all, who's better equipped than a young poet to respond to the young Nietzsche, whose strongest defense was his intoxicating solitude, his sense of his own genius, his inner freedom, and finally—perhaps most important—his sense that the essential energy of any human creation, cultural or otherwise, escapes the notice of the age's learned authorities. These great scholars, who seem to know everything, who've counted the disks of the vertebrates and the syllables in Archilochus' poems, can't manage to identify whatever it is that catalyzes human minds and creativity. They analyze the outcome, but are blind to its essence; they study the fire but can describe only its ashes. And as we know, Nietzsche gleefully calls this principle that the scholars overlook none other than life itself.

But there was something else that proved sympathetic to a young poet: the scorn with which this philologist and philosopher treated the state, the challenge he cast at the newly formed German Reich, the autonomy of an intellect that mocked the might of the Germans united by Bismarck. I liked this for two reasons. First, I was of course taken with his mockery of the state, living as I did under the rule of the totalitarian, Khrushchevian-Brezhnevian-Gomulkovian system and half consciously seeking allies in the challenging acrobatic act of liberating oneself from the ideological and administrative constraints of Marxism. There was also another reason: here was someone who came right out and proclaimed his intellectual independence, who didn't fret about the historical stage sets, who spoke from within his own spirit, and spoke, moreover, with such buoyancy and brilliance, whose language was so phenomenally pure, plastic, and full. To resist the automatism of a specific historical reality—in Nietzsche's case, Bismarck's Reich—meant something more than a political challenge alone. It was also a declaration—like a customs declaration—of his own spiritual resources, his personal wealth, which had no need for bureaucrats and political structures. Could I have found a better ally? Here was a philosopher who, dismissing all risks, ignoring all external authorities, not only challenged the Leviathan but did so carelessly, without giving a second thought to the monster's response.

The Birth of Tragedy—I'm not sure that I really understood this difficult book the first time around, since it demanded a far better education than I possessed. The paradox of Nietzsche, one of the best-read Europeans of his day who celebrated, however, not erudition but life itself, could not be self-evident and readily comprehensible to someone who belonged, unfortunately, to one of the worst-educated generations in the modern history of this continent (in Western as well as Eastern Europe).

I still don't know if I really grasped the subtlety of Nietzsche's vision of tragedy, that desperate yet joyful affirmation of our fragile human existence. I sensed, I guessed, I fairly vibrated while reading about tragedy's Dionysian essence, and I'm sure I was taken with all things Apollonian. But I was put off by his jabs at Socrates. I liked and admired Socrates; I had a hard time believing that the decline of Greek and European culture began with him. I remember thinking, What colossal snobbery, to trace the beginnings of decadence back to Athens! But what wouldn't I have forgiven this writer, whom I worshipped, to whom I ascribed superhuman powers and a titan's intellect? I had to put the problem of Socrates to one side for the moment and concentrate on comprehending the master's thought. Comprehending? I'm not entirely sure that this was my object; I read Nietzsche more for inspiration, for fortification, to fuel the flame. That's how young, and sometimes not-so-young, poets read—greedily, egotistically. They're concerned not so much with asking, "Is he right? Isn't he misjudging, say, Socrates, Christianity?" as they are with receiving a charge of pure energy. This is all the more salient in Nietzsche's case, since this "energesis" is contained and celebrated within the text itself, it is the nucleus of his thought and even his style.

Such were the beginnings—sweet beginnings!—of my acquaintance with Nietzsche's work. He wasn't my only intellectual master back then, though. I don't intend to bore the reader with a list of my early masters—I only want to stress that I wasn't an unadulterated Nietzschean. But even though I didn't keep faith completely, what I experienced was powerful enough to allow me to understand all those fervent readers of the mustachioed philosopher who, in the final years of the nineteenth century and first years of the twentieth, devoured his books as voraciously as if no other writer, philosopher, artist had previously existed, as if the prophet, the intellectual lawgiver they had awaited for so long had suddenly appeared out of nowhere!

The more distant I grew from my first youth, the more I experienced the sensation that Nietzsche was aging alongside me. I got to know his later works—*Beyond Good and Evil*, *The Genealogy of Morals*, the bombastic *Zarathustra*, the insufferable, unpardonably narcissistic *Ecce Homo*, the grim, posthumously published *Will to Power*. This was a different Nietzsche, no longer nimble and buoyant as he had been on his journey's outset (buoyant, although conscious at the same time of numerous abysses). The artist's voice grew fainter while the tone of a cult's founder, of a perverse moralist obsessed with settling scores with Christianity, socialism, morality, grew ever stronger. The very concept of life changes its character later on. In the early work it is surrounded by a nimbus of poetic suggestiveness and thus bears a strong resemblance to the gay, creative spark that ignites the paper palaces of smug scholars and the codes of Victorian morality. In the later work it becomes, literally, a hammer turned against his enemies, a weighty tool (for all his ceaseless hymns to lightness) that is monotonously, obsessively overused. He did not escape the dangers of solitude that he had pointed out in his youthful essay on "Schopenhauer as Educator"—a certain embitterment, a callousness. Indeed, they took a far more extreme form than is usual even for such solitary souls. Nietzsche was also apparently afflicted by an ominous predilection common to certain nineteenth-century thinkers (and later to their disciples and heirs in the following century). This was a shared tendency toward drawing large-scale ideological conclusions lacking any sense of humor or any doubt in their own prophetic perspicacity.

I began to see Nietzsche's followers more and more clearly, that legion of disciples intoxicated by their reading of "the recluse from Sils-Maria." The recluse from Sils-Maria now walked engulfed in an enormous retinue: d'Annunzio carried his umbrella, André Gide gazed at him with adoration, Camus took notes, Hamsun worked to remember the master's every word, Malraux talked nonstop, D. H. Lawrence praised the charms of sex, Thomas Mann wavered between him and Schopenhauer, Robert Musil wore his finest suit, Rilke pondered a young lady passing by. What could be more farcical than this crowd of great people surrounding an even greater person. At times it might even seem that V. I. Lenin, that advocate of violent means, the man of action par excellence, who wasn't bothered in the slightest by the laws of this or that morality, didn't emerge from the wooden house in Symbirsk so much as from the stained and well-thumbed pages of Nietzsche's late work. (This hypothesis is not entirely far-fetched, since Lenin's manifesto of the will to power, *What Is to Be Done?* dates back to 1902, when Nietzsche mania had seized all of Europe.) It's true that the crowd surrounding the now-mythic Nietzsche was composed largely of the most gifted writers and thinkers in Europe (and not only Europe). In Poland there was Stanislaw Brzozowski, later Iwaszkiewicz, Gombrowicz, and others. It's difficult to imagine a country in which Nietzscheanism didn't leave its mark, didn't trouble the intellectual atmosphere. It wasn't just Nietzsche, of course; sober textbooks remind us of the neo-Romantic crisis, the desperate search for a new balance between the overwhelming predominance of science, with its narrow notion of rationalism, and the needs of a metaphysical nature that had been radically modified due to transformations in the traditional structure of religious beliefs. For all that, though, even knowing how much someone like Nietzsche may have been—unconsciously, half consciously—awaited and longed for, we'll probably never cease to be fascinated by the scale of that adoration, the expanse of that influence, the fervor of that faith.

All these writers and thinkers surrounding a Friedrich Nietzsche already frozen into legend and gazing at him with adoration: this spectacle is, as I've said, slightly comical, although it doesn't lack a certain old-fashioned charm today. As for me, my Nietzsche, the Nietzsche of my first readings, gave way to another thinker. I rebelled against the existence of so many other Nietzscheans; it was almost jealousy, the kind of jealousy you experience when your friend makes friends not just with you but with a hundred other friends, two hundred acquaintances, three hundred fans. Moreover, I began to read critical works about Nietzsche, with their divisions into periods, their enumeration of influences, their occasionally petty preoccupation with details. At first I refused to accept them. I went into shock upon witnessing an inspired work falling beneath the blows of mere judicious, reasonable arguments, like a great tree perishing beneath the axes—or chain saws—of simple lumberjacks. For one thing is beyond doubt: this is inspired work, written in dazzlement, in rapture, and not the product of calculation, consideration, as is the case with British analytic philosophy. Obviously this is why poets and novelists were the first to do justice to a brilliant writer who may have had his stylistic faults, linked to his obsessive motifs—how many times, for example, does he repeat the word "proud"? But even these flaws stemmed from inspiration. This philosopher with his inspired pen is a genuine holiday for writers and perhaps also a genuine tribulation to philosophers.

But in the case of literature, I'm not sure that Nietzsche's in-

fluence was especially fortunate. I'm not entirely displeased by
the notion that the young Malraux might have praised not passionate, blind action, but something else (naturally I can't say
what might have captivated Malraux had he not found access to
Nietzsche), that Lafcadio wouldn't have felt compelled to com-
mit murders in a rushing train, that D. H. Lawrence might have
directed his quests elsewhere had he not believed exclusively in
the saving power of sex, that d'Annunzio might have curbed his
cascades of rhetoric. Neither am I put off by the hypothesis that
certain extravagances of modern French thought might never
have seen the light of day (or the light of library lamps). And I
wonder then what the intellectual twentieth century might have
been if Friedrich Nietzsche had died of scarlet fever at the age
of eight. I'm not sure—in spite of the charm and intensity of my
experiences reading Nietzsche as a young man and in spite of
my reluctance to put pastors' sons to death even if only in my
imagination—that I wouldn't prefer this hypothetical century
without Nietzsche. Other thinkers' voices might have been more
audible—that of Simone Weil, for example, one of the few
thinkers to remain untouched by Nietzsche's influence. We're
told often enough that we shouldn't place the blame for the
pupils' follies on the shoulders of their teachers. And yet I can't
help thinking that if Nietzsche had used terms like "proud,"
"cultivation," "superman," "will to power," or "beyond good and
evil" less frequently—someone once rightly observed that beyond good and evil lies only evil—the spiritual atmosphere of
our century might have been purer and perhaps even prouder.
And would it have been such a disaster if Nietzsche's famous
skepticism toward the notion of truth hadn't given birth to so
many eager imitators, even in the last few decades?

However, perhaps Nietzsche—or someone with a more

philosophical disposition than I possess might object—owes his belated, phenomenal success in part to readers who weren't entirely convinced by him and didn't doubt the value of truth. Otherwise they would treat his work the same way they deal with, for example, Maupassant's novellas; however much they esteem and admire them, no one tries to shape his life around them or adapt his convictions to them. Incidentally, those who've lived in totalitarian countries have learned to their cost that it doesn't pay to speculate excessively on a subject as dangerous as the truth, and that the genuine absence of truth makes itself felt immediately, and painfully.

Of course, if there were no Nietzsche, Gottfried Benn wouldn't have written certain essays and even perhaps certain poems; Ulrich, Musil's hero in *The Man Without Qualities*, would have had slightly different preoccupations and interests; certain passages in the *Duino Elegies* might have sounded a tiny bit different; Tonio Kröger would have chatted differently with Lisaweta. (Perhaps someday they'll develop a computer so powerful that it could produce a simulation titled "The Intellectual Twentieth Century sans Nietzsche"; many pages of the greater and lesser works of our age would undergo an abrupt, powerful earthquake that would send letters scattering in all directions, the printer's ink would vanish from hundreds of industriously blackened pages—including the one I am now writing.)

There are homes, clubs, parties, at which the name Nietzsche may not even be pronounced. On the other hand, I know readers of Nietzsche who admire him boundlessly as a writer, a master of style, and who love him personally, a feeble, sickly, homeless artist passing from one sanatorium to another, a man so sensitive and helpless that he couldn't even manage to get married. They don't give a thought, though, to the philosophical, timentalism or else openly admits its fascination with force, blood, and the devil.

The people who can't bear to hear Nietzsche's name usually associate it with all that is worst in the history of the last century, with the SS's black uniforms and Hitler's ideology. It's not easy to strain truth from slander: Nietzsche's last writings, with their massive ideological stylistics (we're taken aback, could this be the same Nietzsche, we ask, who wrote *Untimely Meditations*, the reader of Montaigne?), could and must have appealed to the Nazis, and some part of the blame must fall upon their author. This can't be forgotten; the shadow of Auschwitz likewise falls upon Europe's libraries. But we must approach this with great caution and a sober mind so as not to follow in the footsteps of those hotheaded critics eager to track down the accused's address and brand him as an imperialist, a reactionary, a fascist. Thomas Mann always defended Nietzsche against the radicals' accusations, at times perhaps for reasons more sentimental than rational. Now, so many years after the great war, it's fairly clear that Nietzsche can neither be acquitted nor convicted in the political courtroom to which he is dragged time after time by both his admirers and his enemies.

One of the unexpected elements of our Nietzschean legacy has been the deepening of the chasm that divides our private lives from the outside world. Nietzsche's observations on certain elements of our internalized culture retain an astonishing freshness today: his emphasis on inspiration, spiritual strength, ingenuity, imaginative originality, wit, the need for form, distance, elegance, even ecstasy. His critique of historical positivism in the study of ancient Greece hasn't faded, and his assessments of many writers and composers still stand today. If, though, we view his work as a program for civilization, the consequences of turning this utopia into reality would be catastrophic. And in fact this

not to mention political, content of his work. Still others ign
the life of the poor philologist from Basel, and pay almost
heed to his writing, his stylistic vitality; they merely plunder l
books in search of philosophical ammunition for their own inte
lectual cannons and pistols. I have to say that I prefer the fir
group, which doesn't mean that I favor ignoring the essence o
Nietzsche's message. I sometimes see him as a mediator in the
difficult negotiations between reason and irrationality—a mediator who betrays his mission and finally sides completely with irrationality. His work holds, as we know, certain elements of
Enlightenment thought, the search for human autonomy, for example. But they aren't decisive; irrationality finally wins the day,
and the mediator allies himself with one of the participants in
the great debate.

The field on which this unsuccessful, betrayed mediation
takes place is perhaps the central territory of Western thought,
which has spent centuries trying, with great effort and no success, to effect an agreement, or perhaps just a truce, between
reason and irrationality, science and religion, political modera-
tion and spiritual radicalism, rationalist humanism and Christianity, Settembrini and Naphta, between the typical "civilized
writer" of our times—liberal, cautious, voting in favor of impotence over power without fully understanding, perhaps, certain
irrational strains in reality—and a thinker like Simone Weil. The
Enlightenment favored the rational side, while the Romantics,
as we know, were disposed toward the irrational. This imbalance
continues to the present day, assuming new guises. Today we
have a vast, positivist, scientific culture that has almost entirely
been purged of curiosity about the dark and irrational, while on
the other hand there is the New Age with its superstitious take
on the cosmos, alongside mass culture, which either favors sen-

has proven to be the case to some degree. Hence the not-unjustified suspicion that Nietzsche should be read doubly, selectively; with the aid of a well-sharpened pencil, we must winnow out whatever bears on introspection, poetry, music from everything dealing with political systems, morality, and law. This isn't a facile, painless assertion—it's only one step from here, after all, to the claim that the world itself is doubled and torn, as we are, and that we require separate thinkers to catalogue the world of politics, on the one hand, and to pass judgment on art or literature, on the other. In fact, though, this division is already in effect. We reach for the essays and articles of Raymond Aron not in order to seek out his comments on the experience—persistence—of culture, but to learn about our age's political and ideological mechanics. Whereas with Heidegger or Gottfried Benn, or—if you prefer a different example—Foucault, we don't expect commentary that might be of use to the parliamentarians of the European Union. The issue here isn't the small-scale problem of scholarly or philosophical specialization. It is the deep rift in our intellectual sensibility, our very being, that Nietzsche wished to heal, but he succeeded only in deepening it dramatically, and for the duration. Of course he wanted to heal it, since after all his plan for the superman and for conquering nihilism were aimed at creating a cultural totality, new and unified, universal. His vision presents colossal dangers, though. His immoralism, for example, may be seductive—to some readers, though not to me—on paper, or in the imagination of a frail and sickly philosopher, tormented by migraines, but it is horrific in practical application. Moreover he completely failed to recognize the developmental tendencies of European political and social reality that caused this rift to grow ever deeper, monumental, bottomless.

The enthusiasm with which European writers and artists

greeted his work is understandable. It was prompted, after all, not by an apish need for Nietzsche-worship, but by the sense that his critique of modernity coincided with their own intuitions, fears, and hopes. If I'm correct, his reformulation—and thus preservation—of a hereditary spirituality, an irrational, creative, spiritual element, must have proven especially compelling. God may have died, but religiousness would remain (or at least a certain *chthonic* form of religiousness). Christianity and the "judaic mentality"—yet another dubious point in Nietzschean rhetoric—were supposedly doomed to annihilation, but a form of artistry tinged with metaphysics would live on. Transcendence must be jettisoned, but that part of humanity that yearns for transcendence, the energy previously "given up" to God, would prove to be the treasure and foundation for a new phase of civilization, so long as it is turned to earth and not to heaven (all of this is of course obvious to anyone who's read Nietzsche). But who today—besides French intellectuals of the older and middle generations—would prefer Nietzscheanism to Christianity? A sect to a religion? An adventure with uncertain aims to a "proud" tradition?

He wanted to give a name to the unknown. Nietzsche is one of those philosopher-poets who operate precisely in the same sphere as the great poets. Poets, though—and this unites them—don't strive at all to uncover some proto-substance, some proto-element, they don't seek to set out a unified being in a discursive, systematic, articulated manner. They're satisfied with suggestions, allusions, a net full of metaphors; the notion that they should be on the lookout for a single, central metaphor is foreign to them. Poets are vain, excessively so, perhaps, but they can't, as a rule, be charged with the ambition—*hubris*, rather—of saving civilization through the apt choice of the one and only metaphor. Poetry is condemned to live with mystery, alongside mystery, in endless, energizing uncertainty. Whereas Nietzsche passionately sought to exterminate systematically the world's mystery, to track down the answer to the great riddle. Here he was clearly following his great precursors, Kant, Hegel, and Schopenhauer in particular, who was, as we know, both his greatest teacher and his greatest foe. Paradoxically, though, he was also following in the footsteps of the very positivist pedants he loathed, the counters of vertebrae and Homer's syllables.

Nietzsche is not today one of the forgotten nineteenth-century philosophers read only by specialists, such as Feuerbach or that bête noire of *Untimely Meditations*, David Strauss. Just the opposite—he enjoys revival after revival and it's hard to imagine a good bookstore in the Western world that doesn't carry his work. He's read by young people in the States and France, he's being retranslated in Poland and the new versions will no doubt soon supplant the old fin de siècle translations. The right wing quotes him—which should come as no surprise—but then again, so does the left, which is somewhat less self-evident. Philologists and political scientists cite him. A few years back several of the most distinguished philosophers of the new generation in France published a collective volume under the title *Pourquoi nous ne sommes pas Nietzschéens*—a touching, if negative, tribute to the great, controversial thinker. Clearly the layers of contemporaneity still hidden in his thought —in the argument between rationality and irrationality, in the challenge of "life" to norms—are incalculable.

Hugo von Hofmannsthal said about Napoleon somewhere that he knew he couldn't walk like a king. The same could be said about Nietzsche—except that Nietzsche didn't realize that he'd never be able to carry himself like a real aristocrat (in case anyone is unduly distressed by his or her proletarian sensitivities and takes my comparison amiss, I'll note that I'm speaking purely metaphorically). His endless praise of aristocratic behavior, power, and elegance betray him as someone who is more a Napoleon than a hereditary monarch. Although of course he was quick to recognize this defect in others; in *Twilight of the Idols* (*Untimely Meditations*, part 12) he writes apropos of Carlyle that "the longing for strong faith is not proof of strong faith, but just the opposite. *Whoever possesses faith* may permit himself the splendid luxury of skepticism: since he is sure enough, firm enough, sufficiently fettered to his faith."

It was Thomas Mann who commented in his essay on Nietzsche that he was a brilliant psychologist who overlooked only one object—himself. (Nietzsche's psychology would be, needless to say, a separate, lengthy chapter unto itself. It's regrettable, though, that he was so thoroughly a psychologist of *demasking*, and so little a psychologist capable of understanding the enormous complexity of virtually every mental state or condition.) The splendid luxury of skepticism was something that Nietzsche himself dramatically, radically lacked in his final phase—and who knows, perhaps one of the causes of Nietzsche's majestic, splendid defeat lies hidden here. A defeat for which the philosopher himself is to blame, and perhaps also, to some degree, the modern world. Since the modern world didn't wish to accept Nietzsche's critique as he himself had formulated it. But the world would have resisted a similar critique even if it had been far more delicately phrased, if even Nietzsche himself had said, simply, naively—which would have been entirely out of character!—that the modern world doesn't cherish life, it lacks generosity, spontaneity, nobility, and poetry.

4 Toil and Flame

When I first met him—in 1983, the year I began living in Paris—Czapski was eighty-seven years old. I think he'd stopped getting around on his famous scooter by then, and rarely went into Paris. For all this, though, in spite of these two concessions to age, he was still essentially a young man, still absorbed in his painting, reading, and conversations with friends.

I knew many older people. As with so many other things in life, old age—if I'm not mistaken, since I'll only have the last word on this down the line—is largely the playing out of a comedy. Weakness, shortness of breath, shuffling feet—all these are purely physical symptoms, of course. But it's enough to have had firsthand experience of even the flu or a fever to know that if we've got the physical symptoms—as long as they're not accompanied by hellish pain or loss of consciousness—we'll play them for all that they're worth. It's the same thing—or so I suppose!—with old age. Most old people agree to play out this comedy, just as most students casually assume the role of students, middle-aged people behave like middle-aged people, women play women,

men play men, and politicians uncannily impersonate politicians.

Czapski, on the other hand, refused old age, just as he had once rejected his aristocratic origins. He behaved as sovereignly and freely toward old age as he did, for example, to his Polishness. A few analogies might come in handy here. Czapski was indeed an old Polish aristocrat, but from the aristocracy he took only his graciousness, his breeding; he was inflexibly opposed to the cult of Polishness; he treated his old age with humor (although we know from what's been published of his diary that he experienced—like everyone—all the fears associated with aging). I remember how he once jokingly described the conversation of a few very elderly gentlemen: "You know, throughout the whole thing the clearest sound was the gentle tapping of dentures."

At a certain point, though, analogies deceive us. Neither Polishness nor aristocracy took belated revenge on Czapski; age, a stronger force, older and wiser, caught up with him at last four years before his death. He began his slow decline—faltering strength, great weakness, an ebbing spirit, a muted memory. There was no longer any question of playing out the comedy or rejecting it. Suddenly a different power had appeared, indifferent to comedy and tragedy alike.

But even the last years were not entirely desolate. His friends came and read his own essays to him (his eyesight was almost entirely gone by then). Earlier Jozef had asked for other writers, but near the end he wanted to hear only his own texts. This wasn't an old man's narcissism; rather, it was a desperate effort to halt his fleeing memory. Sometimes when I would stop by, Jozef would be half lying on the sofa, absent, exhausted, apathetic, sometimes even with a blanket pulled over his head, as if hiding from the world, very old. But whenever I started reading him one of his essays, say on Rozanov, he'd revive, rise from the dead, suddenly remember everything (no, not everything, but everything about Rozanov), start finishing his own sentences. It was clear that he remembered whatever quotes he'd used in the essay especially well. These quotes obviously meant far more to him than mere literary embellishments; these were sentences he must have lived with, considered for weeks, months, turning them over in his mind like pebbles, weighing them, debating them. They had become so firmly fixed in his mind that to hear one of them pronounced out loud still had a magical effect and drew his mind back from oblivion, sparked the light of intelligence in his eyes once again.

It was the first time I'd witnessed the therapeutic effect of literature—on its own author. I knew that books might sometimes help others, the readers for whom they're a gift, a surprise. But I'd thought that the author himself, once he'd put them aside, didn't and couldn't have any more intellectual use for them. Here, though, in Czapski's little studio/living room still filled with the great artist's easels—now unused, alas—it turned out that whatever he'd stockpiled in an essay, a book, like a quote from a favorite writer could act like a magical injection, restoring youth, if only for half an hour. I scarcely need to add how moving this was, and what meaning it gave to the act of reading out loud.

Before his decline began, Czapski, as I recalled, still lived intensely, working, reading, writing, following current events. He had two different methods for keeping up. First, he read *Le Monde* every day, sifting from it news about Poland, Russia, Ukraine, and Eastern Europe in particular. Second, he behaved a bit like the retired head of a state intelligence agency, no longer running things, but still maintaining his many contacts, who, through force of habit, continued to report on their activities to their former boss. Jozef grilled his guests about what they'd heard, read, seen. He was voraciously inquisitive. He was curiosity personified, the perfect embodiment of curiosity. When he heard some story that interested him, he responded with his whole body. We should bear in mind that he frequently received his guests while seated on the sofa, sometimes with his legs drawn up and his hands clasping his knees. He was very slender and six and a half feet tall; seated on the sofa, he looked like an old-fashioned high school boy greeting his guests, his classmates, in his garret.

Once he told me over the phone that whenever he received good news about one of his friends "he would jump like a trout on the sofa from joy." The sofa was his reservation, his dominion, his desk, his library, his bedroom, his studio, his parlor. Czapski's father had owned an enormous estate near Minsk, a palace in Przyluki, servants, carriages, trees, forests, fields, vegetables, and roses, while Jozef had only a sofa. In the era of which I'm now speaking, while he was still living normally, the sofa had nothing sinister about it—just the opposite. Jozef slept on it at night, while during the day, propped against a pillow that was propped against a worn spot on the wall, bent like a penknife with his Gothic knees aloft, he would take notes in his journal, write letters, sketch, receive visitors—all on the sofa. Above the sofa, shelves held books and albums of reproductions. Books, sometimes still wrapped in their packing paper to protect them from time, remained in their assigned spots for so many years that Jozef would reach for them without looking, completely automatically. His long arms, like a harbor crane, would wander on high, his fingers would tap the books' spines and infallibly (or sometimes fallibly) extract an exhibit catalogue of Morandi's paintings, a slim volume of Hofmannsthal's poems, a collection of Milosz's essays, Simone Weil's letters, Stanislaw Brzozowski's *Diary*. If, however, the book he sought was located on the top shelf, just below the ceiling, Jozef would stand on the sofa, even taller, tall and wobbling on the mattress's soft foundations, and then I—and probably every other visitor who witnessed this— feared that this ninety-year-old gymnast would collapse. But he was on his estate, nothing could harm him on the sofa that had replaced the palace in Przyluki. He was safe in his soft castle.

There was nothing insulting about this diminution, and he didn't feel impoverished, not in the least, the sofa truly became a palace: his towers were Morandi's bottles, one of Herbert's poems formed the roof, his stairways were composed of Malraux's bloated tomes on art, and the garden was replaced by two windows, beyond which swayed the boughs of French chestnut trees.

The sofa and the scooter (which no longer existed by the time I got to know Czapski)—this was his estate, all that remained to this descendant of European aristocrats. If by chance any well-to-do reader of my text should feel his heart contract, a reflexive pang of pity for the indigent aristocrat, I should explain that Czapski lived modestly, but not in poverty, in a room forming a part of the villa-phalanstery-publishing house outside Paris called Kultura, an institution whose founder and director, Jerzy Giedroyc, was ten years younger than Jozef. He lived in one room divided into two zones: the center of the first was the aforementioned sofa, above which hung the bookshelves, while the second's fulcrum was formed by his easels. Painting was associated with the vertical position, and had to take place in a more generous space permitting energetic motions of the arms.

Painting was linked, moreover, with the chemistry of oil paints, with the smell of oil paints, with their furious staining of bedding and shirts. It had to be kept at some distance from the sofa.

The room's arrangement mirrored the double nature of Czapski's artistic calling. The sofa was his literature, his philosophy, the locus of both his meditation and his melancholy (since if he ever doubted his own talent, his vocation, it was not among the easels, but on the sofa).

The easels were his work tools. The more I come to know of his canvases, scattered across Europe, the more I admire his painter's gift, derived from l'école de Paris, from Bonnard, Matisse, but turned to his own individual expression and directed toward seeing, toward vision: a black woman begging in a Paris subway tunnel; Rostropovich playing his cello; a vertical yellow cloud sailing majestically above a yellow field wearing a black cap of forest; carts in the station of Saint-Lazare; a highway, a setting sun, and a little black car lost in the great expanse of the Ile de France; still lifes, countless still lifes. Once he told me, "You know, you can paint a still life even on your worst day, when nothing else is going right," and since then I've always regretted that I can't paint still lifes on my worst days—some in the style of Morandi, others à la Czapski, teacups dissolving on the tablecloth like sugar in tea, tables large and small (like the last props remaining from the long-gone glory of the palace in Przyluki, although clearly these tables shared nothing of substance with that phantom palace vanished in the past), three jars filled with large and small paintbrushes, and above them a blue-green agitated space, as though the brushes were recalling earlier paintings, dreaming about them, as if the brushes possessed their own memories (this is a late painting, from 1988, called *Shadows and Brushes*); apples and flowers, a rainbow shooting up from a little house and vanishing into a fleecy black cloud; three women leaning lazily, obliquely on a balustrade, looking outward (*Escurial*, 1983); a vase and a white dishcloth, a field near Sailly, a red car, an ad for Morley nylons, portraits of familiar and unfamiliar faces.

So many years of painting! From the early twenties through the late eighties. Seventy years of painting, in Krakow, in Paris, in Warsaw, then just sketches in the Soviet camps, and once again outside Paris; years, moreover, of thinking about painting, writing about art, articles, the occasional startling discovery. His late discovery of Milton Avery is one such example: the American painter followed a route like Czapski's, artistically at least, and his status in the United States was similar to Czapski's, that is, he was a universally recognized master, an authority, a contemplative man of great personal integrity, untainted by commercialism.

He painted everywhere, at home and on his vacations, which had little to do with relaxation; they allowed him, rather, to occupy himself with plein air painting. It's clear from his journals that painting often assumed an ecstatic form for Czapski; not always, not every day, but at his peak, at his best moments, after much preliminary labor, after drudgery, strenuous labors, and failed attempts, he'd achieve great ecstatic feasts, Dionysian festivals—a flame. That's what he himself called his work— it was suspended between drudgery and flame. Short-lived banquets. Moments. But from those moments hundreds of paintings emerged. In 1992 we went to see a great exhibit of Czapski's work in Warsaw; landscapes, still lifes, genre paintings that arose from a variety of impulses and needs, now completed, fulfilled one another in the halls of the National Museum, ecstasies transformed into an enduring forest of canvases.

He suffered when a painting didn't turn out, when, like a rock climber who tumbles from the wall through one careless slip, he lost contact with his original vision. Czapski observed the distinctions between religion and art, he opposed the frivolous confusion of these categories, so I don't want to blur this boundary either. Still, it's difficult for me to see his battle with gray formlessness in purely secular terms.

Though the easels played a great part in Czapski's spiritual life, this doesn't mean that the sofa, with its calmer, more sober and rational rituals, was secondary, meaningless. I can't even come close to formulating this relationship, not least because I—like most of his friends—knew only his cheerful, smiling, contemplative side, whereas I could infer the other Jozef, reckless, raging, only from certain paintings or journal entries. But it's a puzzlement, to be friends with a man who's cheerful, good-natured, open, kind, intelligent, brimming with curiosity, all the while knowing that he has another side, less safe, less settled, more dramatic, far removed from his usual calm sea of courtliness.

While working at his easel, Czapski encountered dark, stormy forces, did battle with them, worked to master them. It's hard to imagine that there were people who didn't see this at all, who were put off by what they took to be his angelic sweetness, his excessive goodness. But there were—Czapski had enemies who became his enemies only because he seemed to have no enemies, he was too kind, too gentle, too wise, too calm, too open. (I'll remark parenthetically that of course since they became his enemies they could no longer claim that Czapski had no enemies, that he was worshipped uncritically.) They didn't see, or rather didn't suspect, Czapski's other side, his passion and his capacity for facing demons. His guests were met, as a rule, by a smiling, thoughtful man, sometimes a little sad, sometimes troubled by something that had happened to a friend (or the drought in Ethopia!), but ordinarily full of warmth and good humor, sincerely and unaffectedly caught up in what was happening in their lives.

He spent many afternoons with his guests, drinking coffee to which he added six lumps of sugar. I've already mentioned his greedy, gluttonous, gargantuan curiosity. He was interested in Poland and Russia, Europe and Asia, art and poetry; communism's abrupt, accelerated downfall thrilled him; he was tormented by the problem of evil and suffering, but his face lit up when the subject was meditation, concentration, an intense, internal life, those who had learned to live attentively, serenely. He had his agents, emissaries, specialists in various continents and questions. He learned of the changes taking place in Russia through Michal Heller; Maria Nowak brought him news from the Third World; Wojciech Karpinski discussed his visits to European museums; visitors from Poland, Piotr Kloczowski and others, kept him up on Polish current events; Jula Jurys, Teresa Dzieduszycka, and Joanna Wierusz-Kowalska described their readings and adventures. Sometimes he would dwell on one scrap of news for days on end—a tragic famine in the Sudan, or the unexpected blossoming of a "poor people's bank" in Bangladesh. In this he was like Simone Weil. Raymond Aron writes somewhere that once he and his wife were out strolling in the Luxembourg Garden in the spring, I think, when Paris and the weather banish all worries and gloom, when they came upon a tearful Simone Weil, who exclaimed, "You mean you haven't heard? The police in Shanghai have opened fire on demonstrating workers!"

Czapski knew how both to take others' troubles to heart and

to rejoice wholeheartedly in their successes. There were images that apparently haunted his imagination, such as the description he read in a book by Audiberti of a cow's torments as it was being led to the slaughter: it put up a fight even with its legs already broken, and finally its executioners had to light newspapers under it to get it moving. This was the furthest extreme, the extreme of cruelty, nature devouring nature, human beings without scruples. And then on the other hand the joy when something happened to contradict this tragic vision of the world. He never stopped pondering the questions that were key to his efforts, ceaselessly abandoned and renewed, to construct a theodicy. These efforts were entirely unsystematic, though; I'd even say he resisted drawing final conclusions. As if constantly awaiting new guests, friends, emissaries, and agents, Czapski refrained from pronouncing his final sentence on the state of the world. New witnesses kept turning up: a flood in Bangladesh shattered the fragile achievements of the "poor people's bank"; demoralized by decades of collective farms, Ukrainian peasants no longer knew how to till the land; anti-Semitism surfaced in Poland. But then other messengers would appear bearing better tidings: a gifted new painter had surfaced in Germany; the avenger Solzhenitsyn had arisen from the gloom of Stalinist oppressions; a smart, witty young man had just arrived from Poland. The court deliberated daily, councils were held, Judge Czapski heard out the witnesses, he was known at times to cry, to rage, to rhapsodize—he had an extraordinary gift for empathy—but he never rushed to pass sentence, he'd postpone the moment of judgment for later, tomorrow, the next day, until finally he lost his strength and died, and the sentence was never pronounced. And this was as it should be, the theodicy was meant to remain incomplete. This wasn't a matter of carelessness, laziness, or neglect, nor was this a case of the court's usual foot-dragging, its well-known red tape. Judge Czapski must have known that he didn't have the least desire to pass sentence on the world, that he'd never get it done . . .

There may have been moments when the time to pronounce sentence seemed at hand, when the judge's patience wore thin. But the very procedures adopted by the court incorporated the principle of endlessly postponing the moment of judgment. The stream of witnesses lured to Czapski's afternoon councils never seemed to dry up. The names I've mentioned form only a fraction of Jozef's friends and guests. From Poland came Andrzej Wajda, Krystyna Zachwatowicz, Jacek Wozniakowski, Adam Michnik, Stanislaw Rodzinski, Elzbieta Lubienska, and so many others. Jeanne Hersch visited from Geneva, Dimitrijevic from Paris, the Vernets from Belleville, Milosz from California, Jerzy Stempowski from Berne, many years earlier. And so on and so on: I don't know anything about some of his visitor-witnesses, many had died before I came to know Czapski, he never mentioned others—but it's not my purpose to compile a complete or comprehensive list of Czapski's friends. I'm sure, though, that he spoke to each of them in his particular way, that is, cutting straight to the chase, jettisoning mere pleasantries and small talk, conducting his endless investigation in the matter of the world. And I couldn't have been the only one to fall under his spell; other pilgrims must have admired him as I did (Jeanne Hersch said: "*Peintre, écrivain, dessinateur Czapski est aussi un être exceptionnel*"), others must have been drawn to him as though to a wellspring, a source. I've used the metaphor of the judge in part because Czapski was beyond a doubt one of those thirty-six righteous men in whose watchful presence the Hassidim believe. And also because the righteous judge can't pass judgment, he never knows enough, the witnesses are always insufficient, new facts are always turning up. Just as the judge is making his deliberations one person kills another, while elsewhere a different person saves someone, and the judge will learn of this only next week, or perhaps next month, next year. He can't pass judgment on time, time eludes the nets of justice, flows forward, craves change.

Why must a painter judge the world? Where does he pick up such outrageous notions? Who'd given this old emigrant living in suburban Maisons-Laffitte—who knows what sort of passport he had, if his situation was even legal, or as the clerks at the French prefectures say, *régulière*—permission to pass judgment on the whole of being? But those who knew him had no doubts. I open the catalogue for a large exhibit of Czapski's paintings to discover the lovely text of a writer from Lausanne whom I've never met, Jean-Louis Kuffer. And I realize immediately that Jean-Louis Kuffer admires Czapski in precisely the same way that Adam Michnik and Jeanne Hersch and Andrzej Wajda do. Admiration for Czapski was ordinarily two- or even threefold: admiration for the painter, for the writer, the author of essays and memoirs, and finally, for the man himself, for his simplicity, intelligence, and goodness. Everyone who met him knew instantly that this was one of the Righteous Ones. And this gave him the right to pass judgment, the right he never exercised, as I said, since he never pronounced sentence. He did have days when the world's cruelty dealt him what seemed a final blow, when his face grew gray from indignation and fatigue. But other times he'd be enchanted by something he'd read or seen, he'd fall beneath the spell of a landscape's beauty, or one of Cioran's piercing aphorisms, or a reproduction of a Matisse or a Soutine, and his words would fill with joy. Since if he was a judge, he judged not isolated occurrences, not incidents from the police blotter, and not even only historical events, but the world as such, and hence the age's interior life as well, its books and paintings, its music, and even its landscapes and trees, commuters' faces on suburban trains, the faces of people glimpsed in cafés.

Here for example is an excerpt from his diaries: "A café. A fat woman in front of me wearing a cobalt dress tinged with violet, badly washed hair curled into little ringlets. Powerful, tanned arms. A man in glasses with a face like a lamp and small eyes by a table on a sofa of Venetian rose. Across from him my head in a mirror with hair like Ben-Gurion's. A tired face with harsh streaks leading down from the nose, cheekbones, sharp hobnails for eyes, the kind of complexion that's always almost magenta. *Ce corps qui est à moi et qui n'est pas moi.* The top part of the mirror grows more and more pinkish-brown. Splendid; the top of my face grows even rosier from ruddiness of the shutters shielding the café from the sun." Obviously this judge, who was also a painter, above all a painter, judged and observed himself as well, unlike those other judges who judge others exclusively and lose sight of themselves as soon as they don the wigs that transform them into wax figures, bodiless and passionless, so that they can't see themselves.

There was one other subject, of a biographical nature, which, to be sure, didn't resolve anything, didn't necessitate anything, didn't determine anything, but for all that couldn't help working on the imaginations of Czapski and his friends. He had escaped death time after time in some—mysterious? miraculous? in any case inexplicable—fashion. Poles know the story well; in September 1939 Czapski, who'd been mobilized at the rank of captain, became a Soviet prisoner and not a German

one. Readers of history books know that the Red Army attacked
Poland from the east on September 17, 1939, in accordance
with the treaty signed by two diplomats, Molotov and Ribben-
trop. All in all some fifteen thousand Polish officers and non-
commissioned officers were interned by the Russians in three
camps. By the spring of 1940 the vast majority of these prisoners
of war had vanished and only around four hundred officers
turned up in a different camp, in Griazowiec, without a clue as
to what had become of their comrades, although they had, of
course, considered various possibilities and conjectures (maybe
they'd been transported to the far north? to the south? the
east?). Today everyone knows that the vanished officers were
shot, at Stalin's order, by a bullet to the back of the head, and
then buried in shallow mass graves in the springtime, as the
birds were singing.

Czapski escaped, though, and in accord with the bizarre
logic of his biography, found himself along with the other cast-
aways in the camp in Griazowiec, where he gave a series of lectures on Marcel Proust (they were published years later as a
separate book). Czapski's life evolved under the sign of contradiction: this calm, cheerful painter and writer continued to
study Proust even in the very heart of the Gulag archipelago. He
took part in both world wars although in his heart of hearts he
remained a pacifist. After the Second World War he was thrust
into the role of a prosecutor of the Soviet system—he was a witness, for example, at Rousset's famous trial—although by temperament he was better suited to being its champion. Perhaps
the most extraordinary moment of his life—at least in its external, epic, dimension—was the mission entrusted to him by General Anders, the mission of seeking out the vanished (murdered,
as we now know) officers. Czapski traveled around Russia for

several months, talking with generals of the NKVD, as the KGB was then known, and inquiring into the fate of the thousands of officers. The frail, slim, six-and-a-half-foot Czapski, the admirer of Blok and Hofmannsthal, Norwid and Cézanne, peered into the square skulls of various notables of the Stalinist police. They all knew perfectly well what had become of the Polish officers, and this visitor from another world must have amused them. They must have had to restrain themselves forcibly to keep from simply shooting him; he personified an enemy class, he embodied an "old world" doomed to extermination. For all this, this investigatory mission was not completely exotic to Czapski himself; it was not entirely foreign to his own driving intellectual passions. He always sought to reconcile the esoteric with the exoteric, the general. And he never lost the sense that he owed his unfortunate, murdered colleagues, that he must conduct the investigatory mission with which Anders had entrusted him to the end of his days, he must seek out the NKVD's victims even if this placed him in a position that was rather too "official," "hierarchical," "formalized" for his taste. (I suspect that for thousands of Polish readers Czapski is still better known as "the witness of Katyn" than he is as an essayist or painter.)

In the postwar years he returned late—only finally in the fifties—and with great relief to his writing and painting. Specialists speak of his discovery of seeing, of the way that Czapski's painting liberated itself from the doctrines of colorism and opened itself to vision, to the moment truly seen. But Czapski's postwar paintings also conceal a purely anarchic element. Seeing may be anarchic, may become anarchic. Czapski's paintings are the work of an emigrant who views Paris and its inhabitants in a "wild," oblique, surprising, anarchic fashion. Not *Freedom Leading the People to the Barricades*, but a black woman sitting on a bench at a subway station. Not *Sunday Afternoon on the Island of la Grande Jatte*, but three patients in an optometrist's waiting room. Seeing must be governed by one principle alone, the principle of "inner freedom" that so entranced Czapski in Blok's diaries. Walking through Paris like a Parisian lawyer wearing a toga edged with green ribbon on his left shoulder and walking through Paris like an emigrant are two entirely different things. A Parisian attorney walks through his city and that city is stratified, sated with order; the president and ministers are seated on a cloud, engineers and lawyers bustle below, every building comes complete with a price tag, and everyone always knows whether you're better off investing in real estate or gold. The emigrant sees a different city, disparate, disjunct, resistant to the force of social hierarchy. Carts on the Place Saint-Lazare, a worker at a café table, a pregnant woman on a bench—these are more interesting subjects for vision than the president's palace. Vision has no hierarchy. A subway car gleaming in the spring sun—it was raining a moment earlier—on the viaduct of the Boulevard Garibaldi is Notre Dame's equal. (This is why emigrants from so many countries like Paris; they subject this disagreeable, bourgeois town of offices and bureaucrats and fixed social structures to the innocent sabotage of the free gaze, thus splitting it into disconnected atoms.)

The postwar Czapski is an anarchist of painting and of Paris. As he drifted through Paris, sketchbook in hand, waiting for some sunbeam to open the doors of vision, for some stretch of wall, some figure, some color to speak in the language of ecstasy, he was free and he must have completely forgotten about the NKVD generals and their conversations (if the word "conversation" can be used to describe meetings that aren't meetings). And of course, he no longer recalled his aristocratic family and Przyluki. He kept faith rather with Goethe, who protested the bigotry of memory and praised the beauty of the present moment. We live in an age that defends memory, since it's thought—not without cause—to be under seige. But perhaps we're exaggerating our cult of memory; Goethe would doubtless defend the moment's worth even today!

To understand Czapski, we should view him simultaneously at an émigré meeting where he's discussing Katyn, speaking in an unforced, ordinary way, ignoring the promptings of political rhetoric, and as he strolls along the Seine, registering both the buildings' gray and the river's green ("I looked at the city reflexively, half consciously noting the arrangement of blacks and grays highlighting the muted greens of the rising Seine's quick waves"). Here, the public man, the moral authority; there the anonymous figure, no one, an anarchist, an emigrant. Nonetheless, there weren't two separate Czapskis, disparate, contradictory; his inner purity combined these oppositions into something like harmony. The battles waged for two hundred years between the partisans of "ethical" art and the champions of purely "aesthetic" art (as if such a distinction really exists!), the heated arguments that raged throughout Czapski's long life, didn't particularly bother him. Or maybe they did—he didn't turn a blind eye, after all, to contemporary schisms and polemics, he mentions them in his sketches and journals—but he resolved this particular dilemma in a completely original way.

The purely aesthetic element in art compelled him; in the history of Polish art and aesthetics, it's easy to place Czapski unequivocally among the opponents of "patriotic," "engaged" art, that is, art driven by its subject, not by *peinture* but by painterly *écriture*. In this he is a pupil of *l'école de Paris* and the great artists of the past, a pupil of Rembrandt and Zurbarán, Vermeer and Morandi. But this is only part of the story. The late Czapski in particular thinks and paints with the dictum "to express the world's terror" constantly in mind—and this is more philosophical than aesthetic. The sweetness of the first impressionists was foreign to him; he found expressionism compelling precisely because it rubbed up against the "world's terror." Moreover, every reader of Czapski's journals—which are slowly emerging from his almost unreadable notebooks to become his magnum opus—know the strata from which his painting and writing grow. They come from an abundant inner life, a spirituality suspended between pure seeing and the anticipation of a mystical calm; but they also address the horror of history and nature. In considering a personality so rich, so complex, so indefatigable in its quest for an elusive truth, it's a bit pedantic, even comical, to draw a line between the "ethical" and the "aesthetic." Still, the antagonism—more or less acute—between the ecstatic and moralistic elements of art is not simply an academic invention. Czapski's solution—I use the term reluctantly, since Czapski was always far more engaged by the chase than by its conclusion—depended in the final analysis upon an exceptionally simple juxtaposition (as befits his favorite adverb, "simply"). He combined a mystic's temperament, anticipating those visionary experiences that require months, even years of lying low, with an absolute, active integrity in the outside world, in his dealings with others, a sense of justice so obvious and omnipotent that it required no outlet in writing. *Incorruptible*, Czapski? Absolutely—but unlike Robespierre, he never imposed the terror of his virtue upon others.

Restraint combined with goodness. Since he was also— "simply"—a very good person, who kept friends not just for the sake of conversation but, perhaps chiefly, in order to help them when they needed it. By the time I knew him, he no longer had the strength to help actively—but in the letters of Jean Colin, for example, I found the image of Jozef "delivering packages to friends around Paris." Sometimes afterward he would sigh—in his top secret diaries—that he was too busy for painting, reading, thinking. He treated the other activities, though, as obligations beyond discussion.

Czapski was a genuinely great person, but the very notion of greatness embarrasses and upsets us. The theoretical apparatus provided by contemporary philosophy doesn't lend itself to the apprehension of greatness. Czapski's ruthless honesty also gave him grief: he was constantly testing to see if his experiences were real, if those great moments of illumination weren't simply a diversionary ploy undertaken by his glands and hormones. And he was never triumphantly certain of either his painting or his prose. For all this, though, the prevailing mood of Czapski's diaries is very different from what we find in the famed quest for authenticity conducted by the caustic existentialists. The tone of his passionate hunt for truth is almost naive—"almost" but never completely. Czapski's allegiance to the tradition of oil painting was likewise "almost" naive. He rejected those thousands of ultramodern innovations that have in our times very nearly displaced canvas, brush, and oil paint, that extraordinary, protean substance, amorphous, flaking from the surfaces of so many great paintings, oil paint, the world's backbone. An almost naive allegiance, an almost naive quest—never, though, descending into the tawdry, commonplace naïveté displayed by those traditionalists devoid of inner discipline. For Czapski, this near-naïveté was a path leading him unerringly past both the shifting fashions and fads of avant-garde art and the skepticism and suspicion of modern European thought.

His greatest threat lay elsewhere. He wasn't hindered by rationalism or Marxism—nothing could have been more alien to him than Marxism—or even by the ideological militance of avant-garde art (although this did cause him the occasional headache and fleeting doubt in his creative path). He was most threatened by Simone Weil, whom he admired, loved, and feared both personally and as a philosopher. To put it differently—the threat came not from the island of utopia, but from the island of mysticism. Passionate discussions with Simone Weil fill his diaries. He knew her books by heart. He knew her biography by heart, her letters and the texts dedicated to her by friends.

Once, in the late eighties, we took Jozef—at Maria Nowak's suggestion—to a performance in the Théâtre Huchette based on Simone Weil's life. The actress playing Weil bore a strong physical resemblance to her. And she seemed to have entered her role so deeply that she appeared to be possessed by the same mystico-hysterical agitation that had killed Weil herself. They even had to stop the performance at one point since the actress playing Weil had become so deeply absorbed in the mystic's own suffering and ecstasy that she couldn't go on. The production's mimesis was absolutely extraordinary, since the relationship between the actress and her part mirrored exactly the relationship between Simone Weil's own spasmodic life and the prospect of a longer, calmer, less dangerous existence. Jozef likewise shook, trembled, and took in every word spoken by either the stage Weil or the actor playing the narrator of the biographical tale. He responded to every word since he knew them all, knew every twist and turn. He reacted almost the way a child does in the theater. He'd whisper the words along with the actors, even jump up from his seat as if he wanted to leap onstage and save

Simone Weil from the disasters awaiting her. The Spanish Civil War was among the most dramatic events both in Weil's life and in the play. Jozef was especially taken by the tale—he clearly knew it, remembered it—of a fifteen-year-old soldier in Franco's army who'd been captured by Weil's division. The commanding officer gave him an ultimatum: either to renounce his loyalty to Franco or be shot in short order. The boy chose death. (This was when Weil began to doubt the justness of the Republican cause.) Then came a brief moment of respite; they reenacted the famous episode, taken from Gustave Thibon, when Weil becomes absorbed in contemplating the Rodan Valley. Then Weil's death in Great Britain began to draw ever closer; the narrator was about to pronounce de Gaulle's verdict on Weil (*Elle est folle*, she's crazy), but Jozef broke in, leaped from his seat, to the actors' and spectators' astonishment, and cried with deep feeling: *Elle est folle.*

Elle est folle, Czapski yelled in the little auditorium of the Théâtre Huchette in the Latin Quarter, and his impassioned cry contained the emotions of many years, the passions of his endless struggle with Simone Weil. For a brief moment, I think Czapski wanted to agree with de Gaulle, who may have been a lunatic himself as far as the British were concerned, but who had enough common sense and political cynicism to see that Simone Weil's plan of forming brigades of nurses on the front line who would risk death alongside the infantry (another of her death fantasies) was impractical. *Elle est folle*; I never found this outburst in Czapski's diaries, but it would surely have surfaced if their author had recorded all his moments of anger and rebellion against the imperious Frenchwoman. After all, she wouldn't let him paint! The painter Czapski wasn't supposed to paint, since painting was a prime instance of a misguided imagination. Imagination—that *combleuse du vide*, in Weil's phrase—fills the void, the void through which God might otherwise speak to us. The imagination is a stopper that keeps us from reaching eternity. Pascal had already denounced painting: *Quelle vanité que la peinture qui attire l'admiration par la ressemblance des choses dont on n'admire pas les originaux.* Art is a pastime for frivolous individuals with inflated egos who seek the world's acclaim. The world—for Pascal and his friends from Port Royal—is the domain of vanity, amusement (*divertissement*), and art becomes a particle of that treacherous terrain from which we should withdraw into prayer, religious meditation. Simone Weil was in many respects Pascal's faithful student, faithful and severe, ill disposed to the imagination. Both Pascal and Weil—the time that divides their biographies seems almost meaningless—mistrust art. It is mere exercises in vanity, narcissism, great balloons in which our self-esteem parades. Weil makes exceptions for Gregorian chants, in which the "I" really does vanish entirely, bulldozed by the monks' monotonous voices, and for "English poetry," by which she means, not English poetry in its entirety, but a few metaphysical poets. In a famous letter to the editors of *Cahiers du Sud*, Weil attacks French interwar literature, particularly surrealism, both for ignoring the fundamental distinction between good and evil and for indulging the pleasures of the imagination. Instead of searching for true, divine, reality, writers invent an artificial reality, artificial fogs.

Elle est folle, some readers will say, along with de Gaulle and Czapski leaping from his seat. How can we discard art and its instrument, imagination? What would remain after casting off imagination? And in the name of what? Mystical expectations that, some might say, are ridiculous in any case, doomed to defeat from the start, since they're false, completely ungrounded, or at best, others might add, inexpressible. They may be authentic, even vital, but they can't be voiced in human speech. Mystical experience can't be communicated. If it could, not a single atheist or agnostic would remain on the planet, they'd all be swept up in a great flow of religious fervor. But in fact, mystics are mute, or they speak in allusions, they summon metaphors, they circle the burning bonfire without being fire themselves. They speak only to those who've undergone like revelations, who've been awakened in the night by the dry flame of God's presence. But art lives differently, more forcefully, immediately. Perhaps it isn't always so ambitious, it doesn't always seek eternity, it's satisfied with human beings, or even at times with a tray full of pears, apples, and grapes. Sometimes, in music, it acts by way of melody, evokes longings, appeals to obscure expectations, hazy memories. Beauty is the promise of happiness, Stendhal claimed. Simone Weil is closer to the Kantian tradition, in which beauty is understood as distance, disinterest, liberation from the senses' tyranny. Art leads to understanding; someone else dreams up all those intimate dialogues. Thus on a park bench someone smiles reading a book. Someone is stirred by Degas's *Milliner's Atelier*. Someone feels joyfully revived by listening to the first movement of Mozart's Piano Sonata K310, that incredibly brisk, buoyant music that summons us to life (although Mozart wrote the sonata during his mournful second visit to Paris, when his mother died, and the French critics, preoccupied with native talents, refused to acknowledge the Austrian composer).

Why did Weil's ascetism so torment Czapski? Why did her breathless quest to fuse with God bother him, a painter to whom, moreover, the fates had granted a very long life and who could never accept suicide as a cure for despair? Why did it disrupt the pleasure he took in work, painting, thinking, life? Why did he require such anguish, why did he need this friend-enemy? He had other friend-enemies apart from Weil. Stanislaw Brzozowski was one of these, particularly in his tragic, impassioned *Memoirs*, where the consumptive philosopher elaborates his ideas and beliefs, as well as his dreams of a longer, calmer life given over to regular, disciplined intellectual labors. It's almost as if Czapski were punishing himself for his own long life, his struggles in two different disciplines; he had occasional stretches of less taxing labor, he wasn't hungry or sick, so he tortured himself by way of these two firebrands and their premature deaths. This clearly doesn't get to the heart of Czapski's fascination with Weil's writings, though. I'll come back to this later—although I can't promise a complete, exhaustive answer even then. But I'm beginning to realize that I've spent too long on abstract problems belonging to the history of ideas, on which I'm far from expert.

I'd rather describe how Czapski smiled, how he spoke, how he welcomed his guests, the passion of his conversations. I'd rather show both Czapski and Jozef—there was no fundamental division, but there were subtle distinctions. You could discover Czapski through his work, his books and paintings, and through the story of his life. Czapski's canvases and texts live on quietly in galleries, museums, private collections, and libraries, so quietly in fact that they don't even seem to realize that their creator has died. Jozef's humanity, on the other hand, has vanished from the earth's surface forever. His six-and-a-half-foot silhouette, slightly hunched, is gone.

Since he couldn't express his entire self in his work after all. No one can find complete expression in art (only the Christian idea of immortality hypothesizes absolute self-expression). Even so Czapski was exceptionally fortunate, since he could articulate his vision both in art, which records a way of seeing, and in writing, where he managed to communicate his ideas and moods and to preserve his distinctive patterns of speech. More than this—he lived intensively and well. I'm not sure I'd say that he had a "strong personality." A personality can be confining. A personality is what we exhibit to others, an instrument by which we exert pressure on them, conquer them, colonize them. Moreover, people with unusually strong personalities often can't tolerate solitude, since their personalities subsume their inner life. Czapski didn't have a strong personality, he had a strong humanity. If he had been invited to dinner with ten other people, he certainly wouldn't have stood out, dominated the evening. He was never the great wit, the person you remembered afterward as the party's star—apart from his great height and heartfelt smile. He came through more powerfully in one-on-one contact, where you don't just trot out prefabricated formulas, but other, subtler things come into play—the smile, the way of speaking, even the hesitations. Everyone who knew him recognized his great charm. It took Anna Akhmatova only one evening with Czapski in the winter of 1942, in Tashkent—where she and a host of other Russian writers had been evacuated from Leningrad and Moscow—to fall in love with him. She wrote a poem about their meeting, and not long ago I heard that Brodsky, after seeing a photograph of Czapski for the first time, commented: "Now I know why Anna Andreevna fell in love with him; he had a White Guard charm."

So he didn't have a strong personality in the sense of commanding attention in a social setting. Now and then he'd even withdraw from the conversation completely; there are famous instances—in the later, Maisons-Laffitte period—when he'd send dull visitors packing, those dreary guests who came to gape at "the great Czapski." The passion for sketching and jotting thoughts in the notebooks he always carried with him was another form of social reserve. But he was not at all like Musil's "man without qualities." He didn't lack qualities (I'm trying to describe them now!), but they emerged quietly. They resembled a canvas stretched taut on a huge hoop and thus nearly transparent. The hoop was made up of Czapski's vast, ambitious plans, projects, and labors, which constantly reenergized his inner life, leaving little space for pure psyche.

I regret not having recorded more of what Jozef said. Now, looking over my meager notes, what strikes me most is the intellectual tension in which he lived, the constant sense of the "world's terror" I've already mentioned. Once I remember praising an essay written by one of our acquaintances in a conversation with Jozef. His reaction: "Yes, but you don't feel that the text was written facing the abyss." Another time we were both at the house of a mutual friend, a famous writer. Jozef listened for a while to our discussion on the subject of the Zeitgeist and its relentless influence on art and thought, then exploded: "I don't understand a word, what's all this about the Zeitgeist, what counts is staying true to your own vision, end discussion!" Of course he was right. Sometimes the idea of the world's cruelty nearly paralyzed him; once he said, "You know, instead of 'We shall gather at the river,' they should just sing 'we're devouring each other.'" For all that, though, he was serene and sometimes even happy. In anyone else, this might have been taken for hypocrisy: look at this cheerful old man in his tidy room, well fed, with friends, and he pretends to be put out by others' troubles. He shouts that the world is cruel while pouring sugar in his coffee; he's not rich, but he doesn't want for anything: Mrs. Janina makes his dinner, Jula Jurys talks about intelligent books, Jacek Krawczyk looks on with admiration, young painters from Poznan or Krakow pay tribute. But this wasn't a farce, Jozef wasn't putting on a show, he didn't know how; his most conspicuous feature was the exceptional simplicity that precludes any form of theatricality. Absolute simplicity, the absence of any kind of diplomacy or *reservatio mentalis*. At most, you could charge him—if you didn't like him—with the occasional moment of exaltation, or at times, the easy tear. But this, too, grew from his simplicity, his assumption that we're all equals; even the student from Warsaw who'd come to Maisons-Laffitte to meet Czapski might have something vital, decisive to say, thus he, too, must be given a careful hearing, his tale must be experienced and comprehended.

As a thinking person, Czapski belonged to that rare breed of artists who—though they battle, and believe, and doubt, and care passionately—at life's end still don't know anything for certain. Unlike the representatives of the far larger species of those who know, or think they know, and ardently preach their one, two, three, or four Ideas, this breed lives with the feeling, bitter at times, but also not free of a certain pleasant melancholy, that the mystery enveloping the most important things—time, love, evil, beauty, transcendence—is still, now that they are old and tired, just as impenetrable as it was in the days of their tempestuous, enthusiastic youth. Knowing nothing is not a passive state of sated ignorance; it's not a state at all, but an atmosphere, a climate of thought. I can't imagine any of the representatives of this small clan ever simply coming out and saying: "I don't know." (Perhaps they leave that to their biographers, scholars, and friends, if they even care, which I doubt.) To say "I don't know" would be like transferring to a different tribe, the tribe of acknowledged ideas. Thus they—is there even really a plural here? did Czapski have spiritual doubles?—aren't eager to formulate a credo. They're preoccupied with the search itself up to the end. Such was Czapski, unsure for long years of his own gifts as a painter and a writer. (We shouldn't forget that in both his journals and essays he criticized each component of his identity—"count," "Pole," "Catholic," even "painter" and "writer"— and remained a free man, searching for truth and artistic expression to the end.) He dreamed of expressing the "world's terror," and in truth his late landscapes, painted as he was nearing his ninetieth year, reach the point when anxiety or dread can't be separated from serenity, even happiness. His journals bear traces of deep emotion, of doubt and despair alongside moments of revelation, joy, the pleasure derived from regular work and reading.

The English literary tradition contains a principle formulated by John Keats in one of his splendid letters, the principle of negative capability. Keats thought the poet should live in eternal uncertainty; he shouldn't articulate worldviews, take positions, but rather open himself to various convictions without relinquishing his inner freedom. I suspect that Czapski would not have been at odds with the young author of "Ode to a Grecian Urn."

Czapski, who doesn't "know anything"—what does that mean? A person who read everything, poetry and essays, who could recite Polish, Russian, and German poems from memory, graced with a boundless curiosity about the world and people, an artist who studied painting almost until the end (and quoted Hokusai, who planned to reach his artistic peak at the age of 120)—what does it mean to say he didn't know? I think that the heart of his not-knowing was essentially religious: very strong faith and very strong doubt alongside a complete inability to stay fixed in one single, stable metaphysical conviction. Czapski's religious notes are full of motion—his belief ebbs and flows by turns. He was so profoundly antidogmatic that he didn't even trust himself. He suspected that faith was taking the easy way. But he knew that disbelief could be easy too. On his bedside table he kept the books of Simone Weil and Stanislaw Brzozowski, two mad writers who died young and who "knew." He required the constant presence of thinkers who thought they'd found the truth, since he himself didn't know. But his "I don't know" was passionate, incandescent. It wasn't the "I don't know" of the sleepy athlete the teacher points to in the classroom, or the "I don't know" of an Italian cabinet minister suspected of embezzlement and feigning innocence, or even the "I don't know" of some Eastern sage absorbed in Asiatic oblivion. (This was also because all fatalism and resignation were foreign to Czapski; he ran all over Paris with his packages for friends!) He required Simone Weil's constant presence so as to warm his "I don't know" at the great flame of her fanatical "I know." As a result, his "I don't know" also caught a spark, became far more powerful and moving than the hundreds of other "I knows" I've encountered. This wasn't an "I don't know" arising from amnesia, laziness, depression, negativity, agnosticism. This "I don't know" was positive, inspired, intelligent. It inheres in the very heart of Czapski's work; it pulses in his marvelous journals, in his essays; it vivified the conversations he held with friends and with people he scarcely knew, whom he'd just met. It also—in a different way—prompted his painting. Perhaps it was because he remained obedient to his restive "I don't know" that he was able to paint until advanced old age, always dissatisfied with his progress, always humble before the great masters, open to new modalities and angles of vision in an age when others by and large merely graciously replicate themselves, erecting their own monuments in self-satisfied autobiographies. Czapski's "I don't know" was the soul of his spiritual life, his long pilgrimage. At times he seemed to seek out that "I don't know" in others as well: in Maine de Biran, whose inner integrity he admired; in Rozanov, whose chimerically shifting opinions he struggled to understand in good faith, although he couldn't imitate him; in Amiel and Cézanne. His "I don't know" helped him to distance himself from authorities he no longer trusted—just as he rejected the sectarian Tolstoyanism of his early youth, and as he ceased to obey the aesthetic dictums of the Polish postimpressionists. This burning "I don't know" was the motor driving his quest and also proved to be—although this wasn't the result of any conscious psychotechnic operation—a guarantor of eternal youth and boundless enthusiasm. At the same time, though—I'll mention this once more, since it's both essential and exceedingly rare—this steadfast "I don't know" was accompanied by an equally decisive ethical "I do know." Not knowing about abstractions never involved hesitating for a moment when it came to helping the suffering, bearing witness to historical truth, opposing Stalinism or Nazism. His incorruptible "I don't know" never led to anything like indifference to the visible world. Czapski shared nothing with the mystic who withdraws from history, like those Hindu noblemen motionlessly poised over a chessman while the English army conquered their country (I saw this in the film *The Chess Players*). Perhaps he had his mystical moments, but he was a mystic who returned, who never made the decision to retreat for good. He searched for the missing (murdered) Polish officers when necessary. He bore witness—in the 1949 trial of David Rousset—to the reality of Soviet concentration camps in the face of those fanatical Parisian communists who murmured that he must be one of Goebbels's agents. His "I don't know" didn't concern obvious things, injustice, pain, political prevarications. But in the realm of endless debates, in the sphere of thought and philosophical conclusions, he maintained a child's eternal freedom. And a childlike sense of humor; he was drawn to suffering, but he also loved to laugh. A religious temperament doesn't kill a sense of humor—just the opposite, it shapes, develops it.

He had many friends, who loved and admired him unreservedly to the end. He was in essence, though, a solitary man. He was my friend and master.

The master of my not-knowing. And what is not-knowing but thought?

1993

5 Beginning to Remember

Beginning to remember! While the person we know and admire is still alive—even if he lives far off—remembering remains peaceful, lazy, and pointillist. The memory doesn't yet strive for a synthetic, unified vision. It calmly drifts from spot to spot; it skips from one episode to another like children playing hopscotch. We say: But do you remember the trip to Meaux? Do you remember Christmas Eve in Berlin, Zbigniew's bass voice singing carols? Do you remember the visit to the Hôpital Saint-Louis? Do you remember the bouquet he brought you that time?

After the person's death, everything changes. The memory grows sober and settles down to its great labor. This time its goal is synthesis. It longs to catch and combine all the scraps and pieces it recalls, along with the thoughts they inspired, into a single portrait. In the first weeks and months after the loss of a great friend the memory repeats: it's still too soon, I still can't see, let's wait a bit. But then the first anniversary of the death draws near, time swims past like an Olympic freestyler and suddenly you have to hurry, suddenly it seems that no task is more pressing. And at the same time it turns out that we're dealing with an unfinished project, with a process of remembering that can't be seen through to its conclusion. Of course, you can write down some recollections, reach the words "the end," send the text off to the printer—only to realize a few days later that you've forgotten something, left something out. Often the most important thing! And so on, and so on.

It also turns out that we have at least two kinds of memory. One is intelligent, educated, not only able but eager to synthesize; this is the memory that sets forth large outlines, rational theses, vivid colors. But there's also her humbler sister, the memory of little snapshots, fleeting instants, a single-use camera producing atoms of recollection, which are not only unsuitable for enlargement and standardization, but even take pride in their absolutely idiomatic nature. And it is this memory—small, quick, acute—that refuses death, will not agree to alter completely its system for archiving recollections. And thanks to this, it retains more life, more freshness in its flashes. It keeps repeating: remember, remember, remember . . . and after each "remember" another slide from its vast repository lights up. It's useless, though, to request a specific moment, a specific day. This memory is as capricious as a librarian who thinks her paycheck is a disgrace and takes her revenge on innocent supplicants by pulling from the files only those photos that strike her fancy.

The mystery that every powerful personality conceals doesn't open up before us simply because the person who bore that mystery is no longer living. We saw the greatness of the person who died during his lifetime. We also saw his weaknesses and didn't dare to link them with his virtues, or perhaps we didn't know how. Now, when the biographical parentheses contain an implacable second date, we try to understand both one and the other.

He was a great poet! It's a pity that Gombrowicz spoiled the flavor of this simple phrase, which is a nobly succinct declaration of the highest esteem. He was a great poet, and as is always the case with greatness, analysis can add nothing to this laconic formula (one may write analytically, and at great length, about the worst graphomaniac). Powerful emotion, intellectual pleasure, a feel for the rare timbre of the voice that speaks to us—only these have something to add.

Critics have searched Herbert's often flawless books and essays for the guiding principle of his poetry: neoclassicism, the fugitive from utopia, the poet of fidelity, the voice of suffering. His work is strangely resistant to critical investigations; it particularly resists efforts to uncover a single central point. It may be that certain poetic imaginations do in fact stand upon a single principle that can't be divided up, while others build instead on multiplicity, relations, complications. And it seems to me that Herbert's poetic world belongs to this second family—even though, paradoxically, the same strong voice is audible throughout.

In Herbert, we hear irony, humor, and that humanist *serenitas* that so rarely graces twentieth-century literature—but there's also despair and mourning. Formally he's a modern poet—I mean modern in the sense of European modernism—but his work is imbued with love of both the Polish and European traditions, with love and knowledge.

These are the points of departure; these are the phrases that trailed him after he'd become an acclaimed poet translated into many languages, after he'd found both friends and admirers throughout Europe, and not only Europe. But how did it come about that Zbigniew Herbert appeared in literature, in the world? Do you remember the newsreels from the early People's Republic (my little memory asks me)? Shot in Soviet style, but trying to keep up the appearance of good breeding: gentlemen (comrades) in hats and suits sometimes pretending to work, shovel in a hand with well-trimmed nails. The apple trees are in bloom (spring was the favored season of the new regime's master builders), garland-bedecked trucks set out for the country while an unseen choir sings; it seems the earth itself is singing. "Dynamism, angelology, distance," as Galczynski put it. Dynamism—vast! Distance—boundless, especially when you gaze eastward. The newsreels suggested that the communist world, just and beautiful, never knew a moment's rest. Even writers signed at top speed the books thrust toward them by starry-eyed readers.

And Zbigniew Herbert, the poet, existed in precisely this landscape for ten years (since something did change after 1956). Anyone who reads the biographies of great artists knows that they appear without warning—everywhere and nowhere, in a small town or the capital, in the family of a magnate or a lackey. It's as if the enormous demographic machine busy producing nonstop our average, not especially highbrow humanity, fouled up occasionally and, crying "uh-oh," brought into the world someone in whom a different light shines. When I think of Herbert tossed into a Soviet newsreel I experience something like a philosophical shudder—how could he, systematic and patient, calm, truthful, fundamentally honest, exist in that cruel express train of history?

Should I speak of Herbert's writing or his life? We're not supposed to talk about the life in our poststructuralist age. But the temptation is enormous. It's true that timid, nervous writers and composers who exist exclusively through their work do turn up—like Dmitry Shostakovich, who belonged, so people write, to the ranks of the utterly inconspicuous, his presence in a room went entirely unremarked. Zbigniew Herbert was without doubt part of a different human family, he was one of those fortunates who radiate extraordinary charm. And those who were lucky enough to spend time with him should try—impossible job! you'd be better off with a camera and tape recorder—to describe this charm.

I couldn't have known him in his earlier years; but sometimes I try to imagine him in Warsaw in the mid-fifties. I've heard a few anecdotes, reminiscences. I got to know him later, but even much later it was still possible to reconstruct his youth. And this was because he aged differently than most people, who undergo irreversible metamorphoses, becoming shadows of their former selves. Herbert changed differently. Time and ill health caused his youthful ego to surface more rarely, in hard times it fell silent and vanished, only to reappear once more, unscathed, as if he'd kept it under wraps. So it wasn't as though the young, joyful, witty Herbert had disappeared completely. You met him less frequently, but he existed, he turned up until the very end, if only for brief moments. And even while mourning the defeat of the Home Army, the loss of independence, the tragic death of so many friends, the young Herbert still loved jokes in spite of everything, he kept his friends laughing, had fun. Once, so I've been told, he suddenly turned up in a large group of people dressed as a gypsy. But even in Paris in the late eighties, when he was already exhausted and seriously ill, he managed to make us laugh. While rising very slowly from a soft sofa, for example, he begged our pardon for his bungled takeoff, "like a Soviet cargo plane, not a Boeing."

A strong poetic talent produces two contradictory phenomena. It suggests, on the one hand, intense participation in the life of your age, plunging into it up to your neck, an obsessive experiencing of actuality. It leads, on the other hand, to a certain kind of alienation, distance, absence. It is a ceaseless interplay of proximity and distance. Herbert's own tomfoolery was one manifestation of this rhythm, this drawing close and pulling back. Poetry by its nature is not an entirely faithful daughter of its age; unfaithful, since she commands a secret hideout known only to herself in which she can always take refuge. Herbert's jokes may have had their source in the amusement we find in the idea of poetry's transcendence. Even minor transcendences stir our sense of humor.

Zbigniew Herbert was rather small. He had a kind, cheerful face, and kept his young man's build for many years; there was something youthful about his features too.

He himself says in "The Envoy of Mr. Cogito"—not about himself, but about his hero:

> beware however of unnecessary pride
> keep looking at your clown's face in the mirror
> repeat: I was called—weren't there better ones than I
>
> (translated by John and Bogdana Carpenter)

I treat these words, taken from a marvelous poem, with the utmost caution (nota bene: the motif of the clown or jester appears in many poems from the Mr. Cogito cycle). I'm not a physiognomist and even the somewhat overwrought Max Picard, the author of the beautiful *World of Silence*, a book about the human face that was given to me by one of my American students, didn't manage to persuade me to his views. But Herbert's face—

in "The Envoy"—isn't the point. We know, though, from the poems themselves, that the author of *Inscription* eagerly returned
to the motif of the clown, the buffoon, the jester, Sancho Panza.

Herbert's face wasn't the face of a tragic poet, whatever we
take that phrase to mean. It was the kind of face the French call
espiègle. There was something puckish in his eyes, as if—as long
as he was in good shape—he were just waiting for a chance to
crack a joke. Even when he grew serious, his face never completely lost its *espiègle* quality. I can't help suspecting that there's
some subtle, very enigmatic bond between the face and the
spirit.

There's also a funny poem called "Mr. Cogito Looks at His
Face in the Mirror" that ends with the words: "this is how I lost
the tournament with my face."

The lovely poem "The Seventh Angel," in which we learn
about Shemkel, a minor angel, introduces a theme that's often found in Herbert, the theme of inferiority, mediocrity. In
Shemkel's case, though, the point is his kindness, which is con-
trasted with the priestly dignity of more *comme il faut* angels.
Shemkel

> is black and nervous
> and has been fined many times
> for illegal import of sinners
>
> (translated by Czeslaw Milosz)

"The Seventh Angel" is one of his poems in the comic vein;
these frequently juxtapose loftiness and nobility with the imperfection of the human comedy.

At the same time, Herbert's voice, astonishing in its intensity, a deep, strong, beautiful voice, well modulated—although

not at all artificial, theatrical in the negative sense—was the voice of the tragedian. The marvelous double nature of Herbert's gift, both comic and tragic, or better, tragicomic, was thus somehow inscribed in his very person, his constitution! He was slight as a young man, but even then he had—or "bore"—that same remarkable, regal voice. I heard him speak for the first time at my high school in Gliwice. And I heard him many times afterward especially at readings, where he read his poems splendidly, forcefully, with conviction. The power of his voice—so it seemed—stemmed from his spirit, not his body. But when we saw him for the last time, two months before his death, that vibrant voice no longer greeted us (although as his wife and friends told us, it was much improved, far better than a couple of weeks earlier, when it had practically disappeared).

I met Herbert when I was seventeen. But of course that first meeting at the high school in Gliwice, where he appeared like a young Jupiter visiting a distant province, remained for many years a onetime affair, the stuff of legends. Still, it spurred my interest in Herbert's work. From that time on, I bought all his books of poems, followed all his publications. My shelves held—and still hold!—*Barbarian in the Garden* with an inscription by the author: "From Z.H. to his colleague A.Z. with thanks for the discussion, 4/25/63." That "colleague" was a friendly joke, a generous forecast for the future, and so it was destined to remain for years. And of course back then this was the only book I had with a dedication from the author, if you didn't count the copy of Irzykowski's *The Hag* I found in my parents' library, presented by Irzykowski to somebody whose name meant nothing to me.

I also remember how one acquaintance of ours from Gliwice, Mrs. K—but we must remember that Gliwice was then a colony of Lvov, and just as the Greeks living in Asia Minor spent long hours talking about Athens, the inhabitants of Gliwice were by and large preoccupied with discussing Lvov, which no longer existed in its prewar form—Mrs. K said to me, "Oh yes, Zbigniew, so he's famous now? Of course I remember him perfectly, I played with him at my father's parties, before the war, of course. We kids played while the grown-ups sat at the table."

For me this was a revelation. That Mrs. K, famed among her friends more for her fabulous cakes than for knowing major poets—I should add that she also was an amateur composer whose occasional pieces were mailed off to various European monarchs and the pope—could speak familiarly of "Zbigniew" meant that she became from that moment a new person, for me at least. It also meant—and this was more significant—that Herbert, like the people in my parents' circle, belonged among the ranks of those who had been disinherited from Lvov, cut to the heart by the loss of that extraordinary city. He thus belonged to the group of people in whom I specialized, like an anthropologist observing the customs of the Brazilian Indians (an anthropologist who discovers at some point that he's an Indian too). With this difference—the exiles whose fates I could observe firsthand, in Gliwice, had chosen a sedentary life (had chosen or had simply been the victims of chance, of coincidence), while Herbert was a traveler. His homelessness was active and impatient, he lugged it like a large black trunk from one city to the next, from Torun to Gdansk, from Warsaw to Krakow, and later, after 1956, when the borders opened up a bit, from Paris to Italy, from Los Angeles to Berlin. If it's really so much of a difference. Unreality may be static or dynamic. And nothing else. He could in principle have lived in my unreal town, in Gliwice, among the other immigrants. Dressed in a dark blue suit and white shirt, he could have gone to birthday parties at Mrs. K's and praised her cakes in his extraordinary voice.

Later, much later, I found out from him that he'd been baptized in the church of St. Anthony in Lyczakow; and I knew that that was our parish church too! But as an exile he was infinitely discreet. He never called Lvov by name in his poems, he spoke of the "city," as if the name itself were too painful, as if all other cities—and he knew so many—required names, and only this one city could get by just fine without one.

When I got to know him better, I realized that he didn't entirely fit into the category of "exile from Lvov," and this wasn't just because he was a "famous" poet, as Mrs. K put it. In good years, at good moments, during periods when he could work under favorable or even tolerable circumstances, he became a perfectly "settled" person, for all his homelessness. At such times, he lived in his work, his writing, his thinking—and also in the history of art. This was another kind of doubleness; the poetry that was of course his chief calling joined forces with painting in his everyday practice. He loved cities that possessed great museums, great galleries (so he wouldn't have been happy in Gliwice!). He wandered through them with his sketchbook, not for thirty minutes or an hour, like ordinary, distracted tourists, but for half a day, a whole day; he'd linger before one painting, one sculpture, and draw what he saw. These sessions also had enormous significance for his writing, since they were sessions in close observation. This observation was aided by his sketches and thus ceased to be the passive reception of impressions and became work, practice, action.

I recently saw a documentary shot in Berlin near the end of the sixties—I'm guessing '69—that showed Herbert at the top of his form, still young and joyful. The film begins with a sequence shot during a poetry reading in the Berlin Akademie der Künste (the German translator Karl Dedecius is sitting next to him). Herbert reads his poems and wittily fields questions. For example, when one person asks, quoting Brecht's famous poem, "Can you write about trees in our terrible age?" he responds with a question: "And what if the trees are unhappy?" Then he's shown at home, in his study, a modest room, but decorated with reproductions of artworks, then in the museum in Dahlem—sketchbook in hand!—and on a stroll through one of Berlin's forests. This short film shows the double nature of Herbert's work very well, the coexistence of poetry and painting. Herbert belonged among those poets—Goethe is one great example, also England's William Blake and our own Norwid—who are torn between two callings (or who, like Blake, work in both domains). But even once he had chosen poetry for good, he continued to require his painting, his sketchbook, long visits to art galleries, and serious readings in art history. Why? I think one motive may have been the desire to construct a solid workshop of sorts; perhaps he feared poetry's vagaries. Poets often look with envy on painters and sculptors, on the materiality of their calling, the concreteness of their studios. Poets suspect that painters and sculptors are better equipped for rainy days, those days that produce no visible progress in your work, that offer no visionary moments. Poets assume that painters on their off days can take up some preliminary labors. Their sketchbook, moreover, serves as a fund of future projects, a storehouse of ideas; it thus has a stabilizing function and provides the artist with support in what comes close to a craftsman's work. Poets fear the element in poetry that operates according to the principle of "all or nothing," the ecstatic element that makes its presence felt perhaps more powerfully in poetry than in painting, that virtually excludes

transitional, intermediate moments, that is like an Oriental po-
tentate who either sleeps like the dead or, on waking, demands
absolute submission. A poet's notebook doesn't have much to offer during periods of drought; it's like a glass of water in the Sa-
hara. What good is a studio without inspiration? This is why the
poet envies the painter. He envies what he sees as the permanence, the security of the artist's workroom, which persists even
in melancholy.

But it also had something to do with "settling down." Herbert was far less drawn to music than to painting. (He once said
to me, joking, "You know, it's always the same in music: first it's
happy, then it's sad, then it gets happy again, allegro, andante,
allegro—it's too predictable!") And once again you can explain it
by "the nature of the talent," by the type of gift he possessed.
But I think that for a poet cast out of his patrimony, stripped of
his inheritance, city, little homeland, who despises the political
system of his native land, the magical legacy of the great ages of
European art—dispersed among a hundred museums, visible in
the architecture and landscapes of Italy, Greece, and France—
was not a purely aesthetic domain. It also held out the possibility of refuge, a temporary home. Siena, through which he had
wandered as a young vagabond—and which was made partly of
the real, visible city, where kids scurry through narrow streets on
scooters, and partly of frail memories from great, distant ages—
offered a week of happiness. Dutch art, bourgeois in the noble
sense of that word, fascinated him with its "dwelling," its home,
its roof over your head, it invited him to stay a bit, to take refuge
within it.

There's something ephemeral about music. You can't see it,
it has no address: you can't say where Mozart's quintet is located
(at best, where its manuscript is kept), where Stravinsky's *Rite of*

Spring can be tracked down, where Chopin's preludes are to be found. Whereas cathedrals are planted on the ground, Italian palaces don't travel (that is, unless some crazy American billionaire decides to drag one off to a new continent), even paintings, though far more mobile than Romanesque churches, have always got to be somewhere. The *Lady with the Ermine* is in Krakow, the *Madonna del parto* is in Monterchi. Seurat's *Sunday Afternoon on the Island of la Grande Jatte* has been in the Art Institute of Chicago for a long time, and to its admirers the equation Chicago = Seurat is far more self-evident than the famous but boundlessly commonplace $2 \times 2 = 4$ (where precisely is $2 \times 2 = 4$?). Once paintings, especially old ones, land in a museum, they seldom change hands. You may—must—make a pilgrimage to see them. You may live in them a bit, you may miss them.

It's precisely because of this deep longing to settle into paintings and old buildings that Herbert's essays on the art of France, Italy, and Holland, gathered in his lifetime into two volumes, *Barbarian in the Garden* and *Still Life with a Bridle,* are so remarkable. (A posthumous collection, *The Labyrinth by the Sea,* appeared recently.) I can imagine that great scholars—and we do still have great scholars—wouldn't get much out of them and might even dismiss them. But these essays are permeated with a feeling that can't be found in even the best histories of art, the most advanced interpretations. Herbert's essays on art are marked by their lyricism. There in his essays we find almost the same lyricism that colors his poems—and that is the absolutely indispensable substance of his poetry, fusing it into one whole. In the essays it assumes an additional function, though; it tries to see, lovingly, if you could settle down in Siena, if you could dwell in Dordrecht, in Arles, in Greece.

It goes without saying that the passion for studying art his-

tory was at the same time a very natural continuation of his linguistic gift. His vast knowledge of art, built up through the
years, was also a component of the broader, universal culture
that was—although he never spoke of this directly—his dream,
his utopian project, as if he hoped to resurrect the multifaceted
artist of the Renaissance. The model, fairly common in our
times, of the poet-specialist, the poet-idiot who reads almost exclusively (and not without envy!) his fellow contemporary poets,
must have seemed utterly alien to him! He used his trips to
study—study and not simply visit—the great European and
American art galleries, to read in different languages, to give his
passions free rein, to sate his curiosity. When I once asked him
what he did when he couldn't write poems, he answered: What
a question, I read, I study, I learn! This splendid intention was,
unfortunately, always threatened by his illnesses. The constant
tug-of-war between these two forces—the will to learn, to ad-
vance, the will toward a universal, renaissance knowledge and
intellect, on the one hand, and ignoble illness on the other—
became through the decades the permanent backdrop for Herbert's biography.

The hard, very hard life and the radiant clarity of the poetry;
the contrast was striking. But Herbert never would have written
—as William Styron did, for example—a confessional book on
his depression. This choice was both personal and part of the
cultural tradition he endorsed. He took classicism to mean:
Don't complain. This is precisely the point of his brief poem
"Why the Classics." In the depths of despair he wrote another
lovely poem, "Old Masters," in which he marvels at the anonymous restraint of the Italian Gothic painters. No, he couldn't
write "American-style," he couldn't acknowledge his "problems,"
share his personal cares with his readers. For all that, though, he

writes understandingly about the Dutch artist Torrentius, and declares emphatically that anyone who demands an absolute unity of life and art is in error. This is one of the few moments in Herbert's work where he reveals the painful connection between biography and artistry.

To know him well, be his friend, also meant being initiated into the battle he waged with his diseases. Viewed from afar, especially from the Polish People's Republic, Herbert's life might have seemed glamorous. His colleagues from Warsaw or Koszalin, who rarely traveled, even to Bulgaria or Slovakia, who spent long hours in Writers' Union cafeterias, may have thought that he'd won the lottery jackpot. California, Paris, Greece, Italy, West Berlin . . . The reality was less impressive, though. Illness constantly paralyzed his projects. Illness and want, since he scarcely ever had enough money. Living in the wealthy, costly cities of the West, he was constantly beset by financial problems. His wife Katarzyna, the priceless companion of his long pilgrimage, would have even more to say about the two monsters that plagued the poet and his wife.

But—let's return for a moment to that film shot in the late sixties—there were of course happier times. Berlin, I think, offered Herbert good working conditions (as long as his illness lay low). West Berlin was a paradoxical city back then, a hybrid combining a metropolis with a provincial, green small town, almost a health resort (Gombrowicz saw it that way too). Berlin was a town without suburbs, fenced in by the wall, and the wall, as seen from within, seemed less frightening than it did from the other side—at times it reminded you of the Great Wall, designed to keep barbarians at bay. It looked almost like the campus of an American university, with its hospitable, nearly empty museum in Dahlem. People started appreciating Herbert's poetry—in Dedecius's translations—early on in Berlin, and it was for a long while Herbert's favorite address. As I already mentioned, the film has a sequence in which Herbert visits a museum, sketchbook in hand; the sketchbook also undoubtedly helped him to achieve maximum concentration. Concentration was a mainstay of his poetry. To look, to note, to sketch—as a painter, as a poet.

To phrase it differently, empathy, an unpopular aesthetic category nowadays—*Einfühlung*, as certain neglected nineteenth-century German philosophers would say—becomes the underpinning of his art: tenderness toward the world, sympathy for both the major and minor players in the cosmos. ("Don't be surprised that we can't describe the world/we just speak to things tenderly by name"—this is from his poem "Never About You," where the "you" is the lost realm of Lvov.)

Herbert's empathy, on which, as on a foundation, he built his dissent against the twentieth century's monstrous history, calls to mind yet another kind of doubleness in his poetry. Herbert's poems are like a suitcase upholstered in soft satin; but the suitcase holds instruments of torture. His early poems and prose poems have something boyish about them, they're delicate to the point of helplessness. But it turned out very early on that this delicacy had nothing in common with weakness, capitulation, and a cover for suffering: it is poetry, or the prelude to poetry.

I came to know him well in Berlin ten years after the making of that documentary, and over time he honored me with his friendship. He had already come to feel at home in Berlin, but he'd also, I thought, grown tired of it. His poetry was still popular there, but we should remember that in the late seventies and early eighties West Berlin was a city of amnesia. Berlin's artists and writers by and large embraced the frivolous posturing of the radical avant-garde, as if trying to forget the wall's disgrace, the disgrace of recent history. They preferred to think of West Berlin as an outpost of New York, a sort of Greenwich Village cast upon the map of a divided Europe. Words—and gestures!—borrowed from the English (American) language seemed to carry more weight than the words of their native speech. Herbert's poetic art, built upon memory, upon tireless observation of the world, at once ironic and tender toward those whom history had crushed, could not be too popular here, there were limits to its popularity.

I remember one dinner at the Herberts'; the poet-critic P, who was a few years younger than I, had also been invited, and Herbert didn't acknowledge me even once. He talked with P the whole time, turned to him, asked him questions, smiled at him, fondly said good-bye. This neglect wasn't accidental. I understood that I was being punished. For what? For my early book-manifesto *The World Unrepresented*? I don't know if Herbert was thinking of the entire book, which he may have seen as barbaric, a return to socialist realism. Or perhaps he had in mind only the two chapters on his work. If the second chapter was the problem, then I was punished unjustly. It was my co-author, Julian Kornhauser, who attacked his work there, while I defended it elsewhere.

But perhaps I was being punished for something else. He may have objected to the undue weight I gave to the notion of the "literary generation" in the seventies, to the generational manifestos that I'd authored, to my belief in groups and generations, to the murky hypostases I employed instead of discussing concrete, palpable things like individual books, poems, talents, and ideas. Worst of all, I thought, with a vulgarity typical of our times, that my generation must be better than those that preceded it. If so, I was punished justly—and very gently.

That penitential dinner was followed by a reconciliation; a friendship was slowly born between us, a friendship always marked, on my part, by admiration. Later, in Paris, our friendship grew closer. I understood that my early offenses had been forgiven when Zbigniew gave me a beautiful tie, and then a second and a third. I wear one whenever I find the occasion. The ties' silky elegance (Zbigniew recognized only silk ties, which weren't to be found in the stores of communist Europe) is a good metaphor for the classicist's friendship. Herbert protested the decline of form, the anomie of our world, even in his gifts.

For two years we met frequently in Berlin, often in—as memoirists put it—the "hospitable home" of the Szackis', where the Polish intellectual colony usually gathered. Witold Wirpsza used to stop by as well, along with the Polish recipients of the Berlin writers' grant: Kazimierz Brandys, Wiktor Woroszylski, Jacek Bochenski.

Herbert's stay in Paris forms a separate, far from happy chapter. The Herberts arrived in Paris in the winter of 1986. This visit was inevitable in some sense. If you look at the poet's biography, you'll see that he'd always—or rather not always, just starting from 1956, the thaw—spend a few years in the West, then go back to Warsaw, then leave again, accepting one invitation or another. He couldn't, he didn't want to stay for good on this or that side of the Iron Curtain. He was disgusted by the baseness—and ugliness—of Warsaw's small-scale totalitarianism. I also suspect that he resisted the ever-increasing pressure of independent public opinion, which wanted to force the mask of national poet upon him. In Berlin, in Siena, in Padua he was a lonely, free artist, he could return to his favorite occupations, his favorite paintings, his sketchbook, long hours spent in the museum, the local cathedral. In the end, though, he'd begin to miss Poland. The West's leftist intellectuals, who would not or could not understand the tragedy of Central Europe, got on his nerves. His loneliness pained him, his illnesses plagued him.

He spent several years in Paris. (He celebrated his sixty-fifth birthday there, I remember bringing Czeslaw Milosz to the apartment in the passage Hebrard in the Belleville district, he gave Herbert a warm hug.) The Herberts' stay was not a success. It failed for a number of reasons, chiefly because the illnesses tormenting the poet grew increasingly troublesome. But also because Herbert's poetry was almost unknown in France; only during this last stay in Paris did Fayard publish a volume of translations. It received only one review; the French poets, who subscribed to completely different aesthetic ideals, could not wax rapturous over these poems. His material situation was difficult. The aging poet, famous in his own land, admired in the United States, in Germany, Sweden, Italy, lived modestly, almost anonymously, in Paris. When every so often—quite rarely—he'd agree to give a reading for the Polish audience in Paris, for the Parisian Poles, crowds of patriots would appear, but things were different in everyday life. In a sense, Herbert's loneliness in Paris in the late eighties was emblematic of poetry's situation in the modern world. Almost any assistant professor who made his living analyzing poetry was better off than the poet; any bureaucrat had a cushier spot; any policeman knew what kind of raise, what kind of pension to expect. Herbert once said to me jokingly, "You know, I've noticed that they always pay me one thousand no matter what currency I get paid in."

At one point during that protracted Parisian retreat, driven by both despair and illness, Herbert decided to bring a lawsuit against almost all his publishers. He even had a lawyer with an office, as I recall, on the Champs-Elysées. He wanted to charge them with fraud, with embezzlement. But his real complaint was that he lived in poverty, he, a poet, a hardworking, conscientious, exceptionally gifted, aging man who longed only for stability. He'd been translated into a dozen languages, the best presses scrambled for his books. Each successive volume was by and large greeted with high praise (the French situation—here he received, as I mentioned, just one review—was exceptional). He'd indisputably been called a master, he was respected, considered one of Europe's greatest poets. He really was a master and he did in fact live on next to nothing.

I don't need to add that the case never made it to court; how could it? Luckily enough, since it would have ruined him and given him a reputation he was better off avoiding. All his friends tried as tactfully as possible to dissuade him from this desperate step (their advice didn't count for much). I also timidly protested against these measures; but on another, symbolic level I took Herbert's part. He was in the right, and if his case had actually gone to some impossible court, it would have been that long-awaited, long-desired trial: Poetry versus the World. The trial would have concerned not money, but the weight of spiritual life as opposed to practical life in its most banal, mercantile form. I thought Herbert was right, symbolically speaking; there was something scandalous about his Parisian isolation. There was something monstrous about this great poet vegetating in Parisian Belleville while mediocrities basked in affluence. Of course the publishers weren't to blame. If Herbert had churned out books called *Fourteen Steps to Happiness*, if he had written semipornographic novels or slick detective fiction, he would have been living in a large suburban villa with a garden just like the self-satisfied, tanned authors of best sellers whose canny faces turn up every so often on our TVs.

The readers would have to be put on trial; royalties take their cues from democratic elections, except in this case the polling booths are placed in bookstores. So this would be a trial against lazy readers, and it would be hard to win. How often, on airplanes or express trains, in the Paris metro, do we see readers with intelligent faces reading silly books with shiny covers? Should we sue them? Arrest them?

Like several other great poets in this historical moment, Herbert stood before Evil and Beauty—the demon and the divinity, two riddles linked by nothing, that create no order when taken together, but likewise provide no illumination when considered separately. Some force, though, commands us to set them together—not for comparison, not for our own amusement, not even for purposes of classification. We put them together in order to discover once more how different they are, and how paradoxically they place the magnetic poles of our age. And yet, standing face to face with this malicious sphinx, Herbert spoke in a pure, clear voice, clear as the glance of the stone in one of his most famous poems.

Do you remember—my little memory prompts me—that stroll through the park Butte Chaumont in Paris? Do you remember the poetry festival in Polanica years ago? Do you remember the readings in Krakow, on Krupnicza Street, in the seventies? I remember, and I'll try to remember well and carefully, since I know that beginning to remember coincides over time with beginning to forget.

6 Reason and Roses

An Olympic sprinter, cheered on by a vast, admiring stadium full of fans, is tackling the hundred meters. Right off the starting line he leans forward, bent almost to the track itself, staring off into the distant horizon; mid-race he straightens up, erect as Mont Blanc; then as he's approaching the finish line he curves back, not just from exhaustion but also in tribute to the universe's hidden symmetry. So it is with the energetic pace of Czeslaw Milosz's poetry. In the early years he lovingly murmurs spells about the mysteries of worlds and fires, about picturesque disasters; in maturity he observes, praises, and criticizes the real world, the world of history and nature; as he enters the late stages of life he grows more and more obedient to the demands of memory, both personal and suprapersonal.

No, of course he's not a sprinter; he's a poet finishing the ninety-year mark, a splendid marathon runner rather, and not at all tired. His volume *This* is one of his greatest achievements. And the stadium was often painfully empty, or filled with hostile or mocking spectators; this athlete had his share of loneliness.

But of the athletic metaphor those three postures remain, three angles of our necessary proximity to the earth, which truly answer to the evolution of the poet.

Stendhal supposedly said that literature is the art of selection, since it's charged with *laisser de côté*, sifting out the superfluous. Wedekind said something similar—and undoubtably many other authors have as well, especially the modernists. Czeslaw Milosz's work would seem to be founded upon the opposite principle: Leave out nothing! But not in the sense of craftsmanship (obviously poetry can't survive without selection, abbreviation) so much as in the sense of his "poetic politics," broadly conceived. You only have to reach for the autobiographical *Native Realm*, *The Captive Mind*, or virtually any volume of his poetry. In *Native Realm*, we find sections that are historical, even economic in nature, as if Milosz were saying, I'll show you that poetry can be made from nonpoetry, that the power of the poetic mind is fueled by ingesting as much world as possible, not by retreating into the perilous regions of inner intimacy. Not a flight from the world, not the infamous "escapism" that was the favorite charge of party critics, but a vast osmosis: this is Milosz's program. It is not a clinically sterile osmosis, though, nor is it objective or even mimetic. It is personal and in a certain sense ethical, and even therapeutic to some degree, since this poetry's goal is finally to comprehend the incomprehensible, an operation I'd call humanistic if that word hadn't been damaged by frivolous overuse in university lecture halls.

Milosz's aim more specifically is not to omit antagonisms. Lesser talents develop a snail-like tendency to take refuge in a hut, a shell, to escape contrary winds, contrary ideas, to create miniatures. As both a poet and a thinker, though, Milosz couragously takes the field to test himself against his foes, as if he'd told himself, I'll survive this age only by absorbing it. Often, though, these enemies moved against him uninvited. If that student at Wilno University could only have imagined how many obstacles he'd be forced to reckon with, overcome, comprehend, how many times he'd find himself just a step away from death, silence, despair . . .

He is a poet of great intelligence and great ecstasy; his poetry wouldn't have survived without both. Without intelligence it would have perished in a duel with one or another of its opponents (since the twentieth century's monsters didn't lack for dialectical abilities, they even took pride in them). Without ecstasy, it wouldn't have have reached its distinctive heights, it would simply have remained splendid journalism. He calls himself an ecstatic pessimist, but we also stumble upon those numerous isles of bliss that Bergson said signal the touch of an inner truth.

In the age of Beckett, a great, witty, and very sorrowful writer, Milosz defended the religious dimension of our experience, defended our right to infinity. The telegram Nietzsche sent to inform Europeans of God's death reached him, of course, but he refused to sign the receipt and sent the messenger packing.

I'm not convinced that Milosz is—as he himself has often claimed—a Manichaean. For all that, though, I see in his poetry an exceptional, inspiring closeness between thought and image, polemics and rapture, California nature and twentieth-century ideology, observation and professions of faith.

Milosz is also a great political poet: what he has written on the annihilation of the Jews will endure, and not just in student anthologies. During the worst years of Stalinism, students read his *Treatise on Morals* like a latter-day Boethius. He didn't remain silent during the anti-Semitic campaigns of 1968, a disgrace for the Polish press and some of the Polish intelligentsia. The presence of Milosz's pure words was and remains a boon for the Polish reader, exhausted by Stalinistic crudeness, worn by the long ordeal of communism and the boorishness of the People's democracy. But perhaps the deepest sense of Milosz's political impact lies elsewhere; following in the great Simone Weil's footsteps, he set forth a model of thought linking metaphysical passion with responsiveness to the plight of the simple man. And this in a century that scrupulously and mean-spiritedly insisted that religious thinkers and writers be perceived as right-wingers (Eliot for example) while social activitists must be atheists. Milosz's model has enormous significance and will continue to serve us well in the future.

When I was a student in Krakow in the late sixties Milosz's writings—the works of an emigré poet whom the encyclopedias laconically termed "an enemy of People's Poland"—were forbidden. However, by employing various ruses, you could gain access to the shelves of books marked with the euphemistic abbreviation "Res," for "Reserved." And what struck me in his work was something that defies labeling (even the structuralists, so influential back then, couldn't come up with anything): its intellectual expanse, its vast atmosphere. Since Milosz, like Cavafy or Auden, belongs to that breed of poets whose work exudes the scent not of roses but of reason.

But Milosz understands reason, intellect in a medieval sense, even a "Thomistic" sense (metaphorically speaking, of course). That is to say, he understands it in a way that precedes the great schism which placed the intellect of the rationalists on one side of the divide, while the other was occupied by the imagination and intelligence of the artists, who not infrequently take refuge in irrationality. Healing this divide—is it possible?—

was and is one of Milosz's great utopian projects, the ambition of a writer who has himself done battle with so many other utopias. He's rarely come across as a classic conservative, though, bewailing the decline of culture in our times, lamenting the divorce of the two forms of intelligence. He's been too busy, by and large, struggling to arrange their renewed betrothal. In the minitreatise entitled "What I Learned from Jeanne Hersch," from his newest volume *This*, we find the following commandment: "That reason is a gift of God and that we should believe in its ability to comprehend the world." Obviously this reason shares little with the cautious notion employed by today's philosophers.

In the same poem Milosz also says: "That the proper attitude toward being is respect and that we must, therefore, avoid the company of people who debase being with their sarcasm, and praise nothingness." No one should shun the companionship of Czeslaw Milosz's books.

2001

7 Against Poetry

1

People who write poetry sometimes find themselves busy conducting a "defense of poetry" on the sidelines of their primary occupation.

With all due respect for this genre (I've practiced it myself), I'd like to pose the following question: Do these subtle, at times inspiring, treatises inadvertently damage poetry instead of strengthening it? Even great poets—Shelley for example—have tried their hand at such defensive writing. Weren't they simply wasting precious time on futile exercises in pious rhetoric? Since what could you expect from a poet but a defense of poetry? Can we really take a defense of one's own craft seriously? A craftsman defending his own territory—what could be more obvious? Wasn't Witold Gombrowicz—a prose writer, not a poet—doing something more original in his essay "Against Poets," which at least prompted a provocative exchange of opinions when Czeslaw Milosz himself joined in the argument? But

Gombrowicz's chief complaint against poetry was its excessive "sweetness," the disproportionate amount of sugar in poetry; he stopped short of tossing it out entirely.

What are the primary charges against poetry? We'll begin with the simplest examples, with absolutely naive poetry, the poetry written by provincial amateurs, retired postal clerks, and genteel ladies who've grown bored in their attractively decorated bungalows. It goes without saying that this will be poetry praising sunrises, the first snow, the charms of May, daisies, squirrels, and birch trees. Gottfried Benn couldn't stand them and mocked the poems about spring that turned up in cultured periodicals every March or April. What's wrong with them?

Nothing—but often their boundless naïveté can trigger a primal and not entirely unfounded aversion. The ability to acknowledge what's negative and ominous in life is indispensable. Those poems about daisies rarely consider the world's negativity —and that's what makes them naive. This might seem a petty objection. Some poet in Idaho wants to write about flowers— what's the problem? Let's admit that there's something appealing about this naive, rather amateurish stratum of poetry. Certainly it's harmless enough, even if it doesn't help us to understand the world. (Newton supposedly called poetry "disingenuous nonsense.")

Even our kindly retired postal clerk, busily writing his glib verses, doesn't live in a state of permanent rapture, after all. He may be a basically cheerful person, but he too endures moments of fear, anxiety, or despair. Can he express them in his work? More than this: it may even happen that this retired clerk is not at all the kindly person that his poems' readers took him for. When we speak of literature's titans, we have a ready-made answer: the work redeems the author's character flaws ("he wrote well"). But does the same thing apply to our little poet? And another question that may not arise in considering a great artist: Why doesn't this gentleman include his weak points, his less attractive traits in his poetry? Is it simply because he's adapting to the laws of collective life that insist that we display only our good sides, or what passes for our good sides, and keep our defects and misfortunes under lock and key? If so, that's not such a problem. Things look worse, though, if the fault lies in the very nature of poetry, which welcomes rapture while rejecting anything negative, which is not free, in other words, of hypocrisy.

2

If this is the case, then poetry is to blame for expressing only a fraction of our spiritual energies; poetry, as we recall, is brought into being by a certain exceptional and legendary state of mind known as inspiration. Humanity does not require inspiration, the companion not just of poets and novelists but also of musicians, painters, not to mention some scholars and clergymen and even those who write (wrote) wonderful long letters, because it's accompanied by euphoria, bliss (although it is). We need it above all because it raises us above the petty network of empirical circumstances that makes up our everyday lot and confinement. It lifts us above the quotidian so that we can scrutinize the world attentively and ardently. It doesn't liberate us from these empirical limitations completely; poets don't levitate, they are granted neither diplomatic immunity nor immunity to diseases. As we know, nothing saved Mandelstam, one of the twentieth century's great inspirationists, from deportation or death in a prison camp. For all this, in an aesthetic and even philosophical sense inspiration does seem to offer its recipients the possibility of a certain leap, a certain purely inward and invisible form of levitation. Sometimes—most frequently—this levitation takes the shape of a creative work, endows it with a more perfect form and greater intellectual power. Sometimes it also seems to communicate itself to the reader, in which case it is like a flaming torch that passes from hand to hand. Such a torch would be older than the Olympic flame, wandering as it does among human spirits since Homer's time.

Poets themselves disagree about the existence and necessity of inspiration. There are various schools of thought. We know, for example, that Paul Valéry opposed the very notion of inspiration and praised only the rational components of a well-ordered mind. Other poets have defended inspiration without scanting the need for extensive preparatory labors, craft, and reflection. This isn't the issue, though. The question, perhaps slightly perverse, is merely whether that splendid disease known as inspiration determines in some way the temperament and even substance of poetry. Inspiration is after all almost purely positive, it is very nearly the embodiment of joy. (We're better off not looking too closely at those it touches—suffice it to say that they in no way resemble those melancholy catatonics who remain in the same position for hours on end.)

But we can't know if our enthusiasm actually corresponds to anything in reality, in the world's structure, even though in moments of exaltation we're absolutely convinced this is so, and even the next day we're still sure we're right. In a week or two, though, doubts may begin to appear.

3

Someone will say at this point (quite rightly): What planet do you live on? After all, the vast, overwhelming majority of poems being written today—and in the nineteenth century as well—are filled not with enthusiasm, ecstatic joy, but with melancholy, irony, doubt, and despair! These days a kind of irony parched with sorrow is probably the most frequently used material in poetry. So it's no easy matter to turn poets into the heralds of ecstasy.

The author of this essay should at this point lock up his modest workshop, cede defeat, and return to his primary occupation, namely the writing of poetry. But the matter may not be quite so simple.

Of course there's no dearth of melancholy and irony in poetry, be it Romantic or contemporary. Not to mention the poetry of antiquity: the exiled Ovid didn't write joyful poetry. The Romantics wept copiously. Contemporary poets no longer cry, they simply endure in a chilly, elegant despair, interrupted from time to time by an outburst of morose laughter. Isn't it true, though, that joy and melancholy form a couple of sorts? These moods are elevated in lyric poetry to something like a worldview, but they also retain something of their characteristic temperament in the epic. Melancholy and joy are poetry's modest, binary legacy. Affirmation and repudiation taken together form a rather psychotic gesture, the "thumbs up" or "thumbs down" casually borrowed from the Roman caesars (both caesars and poets rely on the thumb). And isn't poetic melancholy at times only rapture in disguise, as if the poet wished to enjoy inspiration just a bit longer and so hides it in a heat-resistant container? At times these affirmations and negations may be slightly ahistorical, pronounced without reference to new facts and conclusions. The court assembles, experiences inspiration, and, ignoring the witnesses, ignoring both the prosecutor and the defense, passes its apodictic, beautifully composed sentence. Is Baudelaire's complaint really so different from Ovid's?

What's the harm in this? Poetry's opponent answers sternly: It's not even the inescapable, cheap irony that bothers me. Rather, it is poetry's refusal to participate in the age's intellectual labors, the way poetry ignores everything that is most interesting, and perhaps most significant, in the humanist intellectual endeavor, that is to say, the constant, careful, and rigorous observation of the human world's intricate landscape, in which something always changes and something remains the same. Along with his other traditional labors, the writer's pressing task must be the weighing of these two components, the discovery of new forms of evil, new varieties of good, new forms of behavior and ageless ways of life. The writer evaluates the world, always a little old and a little new, both archaically the same and changing under the invasion of the "modernity" that now sheathes the world like a layer of shining nylon, even though not so long ago it had been traumatized by the convulsions of the thirties and forties, partly under the influence of the same modernity. The age's great intellectual labor, in which so many have taken part, is still chiefly the comprehension of the twentieth century's vast tragedies. Is there a place for poetry in this labor?

4

Why do so many intelligent, enlightened, educated people turn from poetry these days? In some countries, the answer is easy enough; in France, for example, where for several decades the lyric has understood its function as being a methodological monologue, an endless meditation on the question of whether poems are possible at all. It's as though some introspective tailor had stopped making clothes, ceaselessly pondering instead the marvelous Arabian proverb "The needle that clothes so many people stays naked itself." Thoughtful people seeking answers to the most fundamental questions inevitably turn their backs on such dry, narcissistic, hermetic poetry. But elsewhere, in those regions where poetry has not entirely renounced its dialogue with the world, the lyric doesn't always manage to attract those who might potentially prove its best readers.

> Time that with this strange excuse
> Pardoned Kipling and his views,
> And will pardon Paul Claudel,
> Pardons him for writing well.

We read this stanza from Auden's beautiful poem "In Memory of W. B. Yeats" with admiration and we agree, by and large, with its sense. If, however, we stop a moment to consider its conclusion, we can't help asking whether the mere fact that someone writes well, even exceptionally well, really excuses ignoring what he says. Even if we skip over the names Auden singles out in his Marxist phase (do Claudel and Yeats really require our forgiveness?), the tendency we see here is not confined to the author of "The Shield of Achilles." This is the tendency to go easy not just on poets but on novelists too, to treat them like children. You may have said something stupid, but you're so adorable (what a cunning little face). But if we are to take literature seriously, sometimes a work has to be discarded even if it is "very well written"—a large chunk of Mayakovsky's work would have to be jettisoned, for example, though his vast talent is not in question.

5

Is there perhaps some ontological element of reality before which poetry is helpless? Is this the element of evil? Could it be that poetry is helpless before evil? But we have Dante, after all, we have Goethe's *Faust*, we have *Othello* and *Macbeth*. (The "statistical" argument that we have more ecstatic lyrics—for example, Keats, Whitman, and Claudel—than poems confronting evil doesn't hold much water.)

But those who want to understand the modern dictatorships, Nazi or Stalinist, will reach rather for historians and philosophers, for Raul Hilberg or Hannah Arendt, the works of Eric Voegelin or Aron, even Speer's diaries, for Hermann Rausching, Solzhenitsyn's early books, the memoirs of the Holocaust's victims and executioners. They'll turn to Chiaromonte, to the historians of twentieth-century Russia, the works of François Furet, Martin Malia, Leszek Kolakowski, and so many other penetrating analyses. (Whether they'll find the definitive answer they seek is another question—if a definitive answer does indeed exist.) And if they're concerned with more recent, contemporary ailments of society and the spirit, they likewise won't lack for appropriate prose readings.

"Slow down a minute," one of my poet friends will burst in here. "Is poetry really only supposed to be some kind of intellectual emergency service whose sky blue ambulances rush screeching through the dark streets of the sleeping city?" Of course not. It would be ridiculously reductive to confine poetry to such functions alone. On the other hand, poets shouldn't ignore what might be called their age's intellectual debate; they can't avoid it completely. Whether this debate truly exists and where it's to be found is another matter. I think it does exist, though, however imperfect and intermittent it may be.

If poets do shun this discussion, convinced that their minor treasures of lyric inspiration or melancholy are worth more than meditations on the twentieth century's radical evil or on the great sorrow, and boredom, of our times, then they're contributing to poetry's decline, they're helping to erode the high place among human works given it by the gods and the Greeks. Poetry then becomes an amusing hobby for students and senior citizens—not a matter for grown-ups, who must focus on essentials.

It's not the actual debate that's at stake here—it's truth. The one persuasive charge against poetry would be that it doesn't seek the truth about human beings and the world, but confines itself instead to gathering pretty baubles on the world's beaches, pebbles and shells.

Yes, of course. But we have the *Duino Elegies*, Eliot's *Waste Land*, Milosz's *Treatise on Morals* and *Treatise on Poetry*, Mandelstam's Petersburg poems, Auden's "The Shield of Achilles," Akhmatova's *Requiem*, the poems of Zbigniew Herbert and Celan—what do they tackle? Evil, modernity, life in our age, the way our age resists us.

6

Let's take a look once more at the relationship between the world and poetry. Of course there are the rare and extraordinary poems in which a few great poets cast judgment upon our age's ignominies. Isn't it true, by and large, though, that poetry doesn't possess cognitive apparatus attuned to banality, baseness, boredom (I'm not thinking of the artist's elegant ennui, of Baudelaire's spleen, but of our cities' sleepy boredom on an ordinary Sunday afternoon), as well as to Eichmann, the raging skinhead, the soulless bureaucrat.

There is, of course, a certain variety of evil that eludes poetry, that only the novelist—perhaps only Dostoevsky—can handle. We'll call this "Dostoevsky's evil," the evil of Stavrogin and Smerdyakov, and of the young Verkhovensky, an evil that is simultaneously both psychological and theological. As concerns the potent evil of Hitler and Stalin, poetry confines itself chiefly, and sometimes wonderfully, to the victims' laments, as in the poetry of Celan, for example, of Milosz, Herbert, and Akhmatova. However, it approaches the sources of this evil only with extreme difficulty. (It should be said immediately, though, that the greatest philosophical minds haven't offered much more.)

It's not simply a matter of the perception of evil. I'm also concerned with the modern definition of poetry, not the theoretical definition, since there isn't one, but the practical definition applied by even the greatest masters, one that accurately reflects the changes that have taken place in the modern mind. Rainer Maria Rilke, the most universally admired twentieth-century poet, has little to say on a topic that enthralled the ancients and should involve us, too: how to live among other humans, in what kind of human community? He speaks beautifully, though, about how to live in the privacy of existence, in solitude, in solitary love, and also about how to die.

7

Perhaps it's that lyric poetry has two wings, two chief concerns. The first of these is the venerable task that is perhaps the lyric's absolute center in every generation: this is the need for continuity, the need to sustain spiritual life, or rather, to provide forms for our inner life. Since in poetry, as in meteorology, two atmospheric fronts are always colliding: the warm air of our introspection meets up with the cold front of form, the chill breeze of reflection. The "minor treasures of lyric inspiration" I've mentioned rather dismissively (for pedagogical purposes!) are genuine treasures, and their registration has tremendous significance regardless of the philosophical sense they're assigned.

What is the spiritual life? It's aggravating that the question must even be raised; but whenever I pronounce these words, perhaps especially in the United States, my interlocutors look at me slightly askance, as if to say: Get thee to a monastery! The spiritual life doesn't need to hide beneath a Cistercian's habit, though; it's often simply close observation of the things of this world with the imagination's eye. It may also be a way station on a religious quest, but how much of this remains in contemporary poetry is difficult to say: isn't poetry rather mysticism for beginners? The Catholic philosopher Jacques Maritain urged poets to concentrate on the material and craft of poetry as well.

Poetry is an art and thus cannot be reduced to spiritual activity. We need to bear in mind, nonetheless, that only in the inner life, as in a broken mirror, do we occasionally catch glimpses of eternity's small, mobile flame, whatever the mocking (or not) reader may understand this to be.

At the same time, though, the inner life must be concealed, it can't be flaunted in public. Like the poor stokers in Hofmannsthal's famous "Manche freilich," it must be confined beneath the ship's deck. It can't come out for two reasons. First of all, it's not photogenic; it's as transparent as May air. And second, the minute it decides to draw public attention, it becomes a narcissistic clown. But—and the comparison with the stoker is apt here—this invisible, discrete inner life is, in its passion, its naïveté, its bitterness and its indefatigable, vivifying enthusiasm, the final and indispensable energy propelling both poetry and people.

Contemporary mass culture, entertaining and at times harmless as it may be, is marked by its complete ignorance of the inner life. Not only can it not create this life; it drains it, corrodes it, undermines it. Science, caught up in other problems, likewise neglects it. Thus only a few artists, philosophers, and theologians are left to defend this fragile, besieged fortress.

Defending the spiritual life is not merely a sop thrown to the radical aesthetes. I see the spiritual life, the inner voice that speaks to us, or perhaps only whispers, in Polish, English, Russian, or Greek, as the mainstay and foundation of our freedom, the indispensable territory of reflection and independence shielding us from the mighty blows and temptations of modern life.

8

Poetry's second wing, on the other hand, is distinguished by its more intellectual, cognitive character. It pays courageous heed to our world's changing face, it seeks the truth about us, it conducts tireless reconnaissance missions in reality's countless corridors, it opposes lies. Poetry must be on the watch for history; it can't rely exclusively upon private experience as understood by the English poet and philosopher Kathleen Raine, for example, that is, an ahistorical return to the models and motifs of the *sacrum* set forth by a very few poets in the English tradition (Blake, Keats, Yeats). Recognizing historical change, standing guard on the square before the president's palace, reflecting on the gradual or rapid metamorphoses of our civilization: all this is vital too. A thoroughly sober gaze directed toward the historical world thus makes up the second pillar of poetry, which stands alongside the inner experience springing from some source unknown to us.

Sometimes the search for truth takes the shape of a rather different investigation: the attempt to create a common human measure. Each writer, each poet is also a judge of the human world (he also judges himself upon occasion); a poem's every line submits the world to a verdict based on earlier reflection. Every line conceals the sufferings of Cambodia and Auschwitz (I know this sounds bombastic, but so be it). Every line also holds a spring day's joy. Tragedy and joy collide in every line.

And another thing. In poetry we must always take at least two things into consideration: that which is, and that which we are. We must see the human comedy clearly and cruelly, we must see the vanity and foolishness both of ourselves and of those near to us. But we shouldn't hastily abandon all aspirations to a higher world, a higher order, even though the spectacle of human folly may discourage us. We don't lack for superb reporters to remind us of human poverty; but who will remind us simultaneously of what uplifts us? These two visions should ideally always work in tandem. An account of human degradation alone—however scrupulous—can lead only to dreary naturalism. When divorced from sober judgment, raptures over life's ecstatic potentials, its theological dimension, can create only an insufferable rhetoric bursting with unjustified pride. But it's extremely difficult to maintain both viewpoints simultaneously; poetry is finally impossible (just as human life is impossible according to Simone Weil).

9

And perhaps these two wings just get in each other's way—like the poor albatross whose clumsy steps across the ship's deck were described by a sympathetic poet. At times they even seem to operate at cross-purposes. The bee-like gathering of spirituality is elegaic, a purely meditative activity (almost passive, slightly Buddhist) located between expression and recognition, while the intellectual apprehension of the world demands an alert mind, quick intelligence, a different form of inner orientation. They interfere with each other's moods, they search in different directions, they're curious about different things.

In a certain limited sense the two mutually obstructive wings of lyric poetry might be compared to the classical symbols of reason and revelation, to Athens and Jerusalem. (This was how Lev Shestov and Leo Strauss saw this dilemma, with

Shestov choosing Jerusalem while Strauss found the conflict insoluble.) Hence poets—along with a certain percentage of thinking people—are doomed to life in the rift between Athens and Jerusalem, between a finally unreachable truth and beauty, between sober analysis and religious feeling, between astonishment and piety, between thought and inspiration.

10

"How do poets live?" someone may ask. "Do they really toss and turn between faith and reflection?" I suspect that they usually live differently. They live defending poetry. Poets live like the defenders of a besieged citadel, checking to see whether the enemy is approaching and where he's coming from. This isn't a healthy way of life; it often makes for a lack of generosity and self-criticism. It may render poets incapable of thinking against themselves—and against the age, which is generally mistaken.

Do they seek truth? Don't they too easily fall prey to frivolous prophets, chaotic philosophers, whom they can neither understand nor renounce? Poetry's poverty lies precisely in the excessive faith it places in the day's reigning thinkers—and politicians. This is what happened, after all, in the middle of the last century, whose heavy lid still presses down on us. Poets possessed by great emotion, subservient to the energies of talent, no longer perceive reality. Why did Brecht serve Stalin? Why did Neruda adore him? Why did Gottfried Benn place his faith in Hitler for several months? Why did the French poets believe in the structuralists? Why do young American poets pay so much attention to their immediate family and neglect a deeper reality?

Why are there so many mediocre poets, whose triteness drives us to despair? Why do contemporary poets—those hundreds and thousands of poets—agree to spiritual tepidity, to those small, well-crafted, ironic jokes, to elegant, at times rather pleasant, nihilism?

11

In conclusion I must confess (as the reader has already guessed) that I'm not entirely opposed to a free, wise, splendid poetry that manages to link near and far, high and low, the earthly and the divine, a poetry that manages to transcribe the soul's motions, lovers' quarrels, the scene on a city street, and can, at the same time, attend to history's footsteps, a tyrant's lies, that won't fail in the hour of trial. I'm angered only by small poetry, mean-spirited, unintelligent, a lackey poetry, slavishly intent on the promptings of the spirit of the age, that lazy bureaucrat flitting just above the earth in a dirty cloud of illusion.

8 Poetry and Doubt

A moralist is someone who appeals to the better side of human nature, an orator mindful of the primary choice between good and evil, someone who reminds us of our basic obligations and condemns our failings and mistakes. It's a person who speaks like an angel. So at any rate—perhaps rather naively—we're accustomed to thinking in Poland. In France, though, a moralist is a writer who speaks ill of others. The best moralist is he who hits hardest. This worthy tradition was born under the sign of La Rochefoucauld and Chamfort (and the greatest of them all, Pascal!); it is a tradition of malicious mockery that conceals a rarely expressed maximalist ideal of humanity with religious overtones. In the twentieth century it found a successor who didn't resemble his venerable progenitors in the slightest (it's true that Cioran notes with satisfaction that Prince La Rochefoucauld was a timid person by nature). This was a poor immigrant from Romania, an Orthodox priest's son, a typical Central European intellectual in some respects, one of those scribes nesting in Parisian attics whose source of livelihood and precise origins are unknown; is he from Budapest or Bucharest? (The Parisians never ask in any case, since they couldn't care less.)

An unusual book appeared in France in November of this year—the posthumously published diaries of Emil Cioran, entitled *Cahiers*, that is, *Notebooks*, which were prepared for publication by the writer's longtime companion, Simone Boué (herself no longer living). The book caused a sensation for a simple reason. Cioran, the famed author of fascinating philosophical essays, bleak, exceptionally pessimistic works translated into many languages and grounded in the principle that "only he who was never born is happy," suddenly produces what may well be his greatest book two years after his death (his dates are 1911–1995). It doesn't precisely contradict his earlier work; still it serves as a kind of corrective, it supplements the earlier writings in fascinating ways. Cioran emerges here as a religious thinker, a personality richer than his previous essays had suggested. The earlier essays called to mind a scrupulously pruned French garden, while the diary reveals at times a different person, less consistent than he'd seemed earlier, a different, more complex philosopher, even at times a poet.

The *Notebooks*—they span the years 1957–72, so they don't go all the way to the end—were published, like Kafka's work, against the wishes of the author, who didn't want his private notes made public (although he didn't burn them! In our times you can't rely on others, you have to destroy your manuscripts yourself). The book is uncommonly irritating—as it should be, a personal diary that doesn't bother anyone has clearly been falsified. Cioran irritates us with his extreme narcissism (the book contains at least two hundred self-definitions), his ill humor, his hypochondria, his radical misanthropy: he experiences a shock of revulsion at the sight of common humanity each time he happens to enter a subway car or suburban train. This narcissism distinguishes him from La Rochefoucauld, who never wrote about himself.

He irritates us both with the obsessions themselves and with the conviction, articulated on more than one occasion, that great art is born only of obsessions. He arouses impatience, aggravation, and pity—but also admiration for the courage with which he reveals his own failings. But he doesn't stop there; after all, that's not so extraordinary, young American poets do little else in their flawed poems. In his diaries he constructs a brilliant philosophical treatise written in installments and filled with wrenching contradictions, the confession of a woeful, gifted child of his century.

Who was Cioran? He was born in a Romanian village, which he affectionately remembered as a lost paradise to the end of his life. The son, as I mentioned, of a provincial priest, he was extraordinarily talented and began publishing early on. He was also afflicted early on by his maniacally intense spiritual life, by various neurasthenias and by his greatest foe, an ominous monster called insomnia. (Or rather, Insomnia; this complaint, to which Cioran sometimes ascribes philosophical virtues, was to plague him for years to come.) He settled in France before the war, but only in the immediate postwar years did he begin writing in French (he had already written and published several books in Romanian). He soon won the reputation as one of the best stylists in French literature, although he retained his Romanian accent in speaking. A perfectionist, Cioran never spoke on French television or radio; he doubtless couldn't tolerate the thought that the flawless stylist might mangle the spoken language by mispronouncing all the French variants of the vowel *e*.

His fascist episode, a period of genuine enthusiasm for the Romanian Iron Guard, casts a shadow on his biography (in his diaries he notes that "my affirmations only add to my troubles, my negations are received enthusiastically").

He developed an uncanny knack for attracting paradoxical living conditions to his apartment in the very heart of Paris (21, rue de l'Odéon). He never prospered and lived very modestly to the end (although in his diary of the sixties he notes with something like astonishment that he now owns five or six suits!). He didn't accept literary honors; in his diary he notes that it doesn't befit Job, after all, to receive literary awards . . . He was considered a recluse, an ascetic, and so he was, up to a point. At the same time, though, he led an exceptionally active "Parisian" social life and knew "all Paris" (*le tout-Paris*). He was at times considered "fashionable"; he became a specialist in suicide . . . He befriended Beckett (if two such eccentrics could really be friends), Ionesco, Henri Michaux, he knew Celan. Whom didn't he know!

He attended Parisian parties (and reproached himself bitterly the morning after); when he came across friends, he could talk for hours on end without letting anyone else get a word in edgewise. But how he suffered afterward on that account! He loathed Parisian hypocrisy, the Parisian literary industry, Parisian snobbery—and at the same time he took to it all like a duck takes to water. Once, after visiting an exhibit of Jozef Czapski's work (he knew him too, and, I think, admired him in his way), he wrote that the people at the show smiled not hypocritically, but sincerely, since they were Poles, not Frenchmen.

His diary is a hymn in praise of solitude and silence; the great conversationalist Cioran loved only quiet. For all that, you have to admire the diary's honesty. Cioran frequently speaks badly of himself: he doesn't pass over his countless minor treacheries in silence, he mocks himself, the failed Buddhist halted halfway on the road to mysticism, the disciple of Tao who knows half of Paris. But he betrayed only himself, only his cherished self-image. He longed to be an Asian sage despising the minor matters of this world while making his way toward Nirvana or what the Stoics called *ataraxia*—but he was forever wrangling with rude barbers, pushy shopgirls, dilatory cashiers, and finally, with himself. He had a litigious nature but was drawn to the Stoic—or Buddhist—ideal of passivity and inner calm.

He likewise dreamed of achieving complete indifference to the fate of his own books. More than this—he dreamed of giving up writing completely and reaching maximal happiness and satisfaction through absolute passivity and intentionally aimless meditation. Nonetheless he would call his publisher to remind him to stock his books in Parisian bookstores, and he suffered when an American editor rejected his essay on Paul Valéry, just as any other writer would in his place. Cioran didn't want to be who he was; he didn't want to be Romanian, or a writer, or a crank. Above all, he was revolted by the Parisian man of letters he'd become!

He never abandoned the dream of being "the hangman's son" with which he used to shock his friends. At the same time, though, he led the thoroughly correct life of a bourgeois intellectual. He wanted to be demonically other, but without effort (he didn't wish to torture himself, or others, like de Sade or Artaud). He would have preferred to inherit infamy from his parents the way others inherit the color of their eyes. Other people dream of receiving a fortune, he longed for a family disgrace.

He admired Simone Weil and they shared a certain secret

similarity; both were drawn to "decreation," that is, the dissolution of—their own—existence. Suicide was Cioran's greatest philosophical obsession. At times he dealt with it pragmatically and wrote that those who think about killing themselves never actually do it. Opposites in so many respects—the selfish, lazy (in the Eastern style) Cioran versus Weil the tireless activist serving the oppressed—both saw themselves as hampering God.

"My son would undoubtably be a murderer," the childless Cioran commented. But he also told a friend who was soon to become a father that he was taking a monstrous risk: "Your son may become a murderer." The continuation of life on earth struck him as insanity, and each new pregnancy was a mistake.

"I go to my Doubt each day the way other people go to the office," he wrote once in his diary. Diary writing stands under the sign of Doubt, written—in this passage—with a capital letter. The great prompter of doubt is death. Why—why should I do this or that, think this or that, say this or that, when death will come inevitably? Friends' funerals were torture for Cioran; a cremation at Père Lachaise acts on him more forcibly than all his readings of ancient skeptics and cynics. Yet sometimes there's a certain majesty in this as well; even an insignificant neighbor whose loud radio had bothered the writer for years undergoes an exceptional metamorphosis in death. Thus we discover the baroque Cioran, who lives constantly with the thought of death; and insomnia stands revealed as death's cousin, its emissary.

The official world, both political and academic, has been infected by lies; truth lives only in doubt, in opposition, in solitude, in an anarchistic relationship to life. It's not difficult to discern in this a trace of the writer's very private resentment. His early, misguided support of Romanian fascism (a ghastly mistake committed by so many prominent Romanian intellectuals, not just by Cioran) surely led him to shun any form of affirmation. Once bitten . . . To interpret Cioran this way—and it's an easy reading, a little obvious, too easy—deprives him of much of his dark charm, reduces him automatically to "one of many" intellectuals.

But Cioran's drama can be interpreted differently, more individually, as the record of a single, distinctive soul; the story of his love for poetry forms one thread in this thousand-page book. In a nutshell—it is the story of poetry slowly being strangled by skepticism, by doubt. Cioran has his favorite poets: Dickinson, Shelley, Dowson. But he turns to them ever more rarely, grows ever further from poetry. He can't bear Rilke's letters, and prefers the cynicism in some of Gottfried Benn's letters. Poetry's rival is bitter, mocking, illusionless prose. The only poet who speaks to him in the end is Johann Sebastian Bach. Bach's music always astounds him, commands him to cross to the other side, the side of joy, affirmation, and God (only Handel's *Messiah* has a comparable effect). But just for a moment.

In the diary, Cioran becomes exceptionally laconic whenever moments of poetry appear—as signaled by music or long walks in the lonely landscapes of the French countryside. Doubt, on the other hand, is eloquent; urged on by the author's voice, Doubt's pronouncements cut the way Spinoza cut lenses. Cioran's diary is essentially a platform designed for Doubt's benefit. In the diary, poetry leads a marginal, almost conspiratorial existence; it dwindles and fades. But even its modest presence lends Cioran's posthumously published book the charm of novelty, since precisely this love affair with poetry and music permits us to revise our earlier portrait, derived from the essays, of the Parisian misanthrope.

Another book appeared this year in September that would seem to have nothing in common with Cioran's bloated tome, namely Czeslaw Milosz's *Roadside Dog*, a marvelous collection of short prose pieces and poems. Nothing in common? Let's see if we can't turn up something . . .

In the first place, the authors are contemporaries, representatives of the same generation: Milosz is only three months younger than Cioran. They must have bumped into each other in the Paris of the fifties. Furthermore, *Roadside Dog*, while not a diary, is "diary-like," a loosely structured, open-ended book. It is also philosophical, even metaphysical; like Cioran's work, it is a treatise on our world. The resources of memory and experience both writers command are likewise not entirely disparate. Both came to Paris, the City of Light, from the dangerous, uncertain territories of Eastern Europe (although Cioran experienced the Nazi occupation only in its ameliorated French version). Even philosophically speaking, it's possible to come up with certain similarities between them. Still, it's difficult to imagine two more different books. The raw material may be similar in both cases: the aversion to utopias, the fascination with religion, the ruthless criticism of Parisian and Western intellectual fads, spiritual independence, the sense both of distance from and, often enough, superiority to their Western intellectual associates. But the existential treatment given this material is diametrically different.

Roadside Dog and Cioran's *Notebooks*—when examined up close—are like two still lifes. In one, Milosz's work, you see a splendid apple and a gleaming oyster in the foreground, and only by peering deep into the background will you glimpse the indistinct silhouette of a guillotine. In Cioran's picture, on the other hand, pride of place is given to a bare skull and a thin stream of sand trickling through an elegant hourglass that blocks a bunch of grapes. (Though it's true that in baroque iconography an apple also signifies transience . . .)

Roadside Dog is, however, a very particular kind of picture. Its author wanted to show us what he ordinarily reveals only reluctantly: the canvas's dark side, the author's knowledge of terror, the horror of the Soviet death machine, but also the extermination that faces every living being. Milosz's treatise on reality is, for all that, a serene work, the work of a classicist who masters the world's horror not by forgetting it, but rather by feeding upon it in his own way. Despair and doubt are conquered not by classicism alone, after all—that would be too weak a medicine for reality's evil! Only poetry, that indefinable something that blends together joy and grief like oxygen and nitrogen. Poetry, that tiny grain of rapture that changes the world's flavor. Like Milosz's earlier work, *Roadside Dog* is like a scale in whose pans lie horror and beauty. And if beauty almost always triumphs, this is due not to some abstract humanism, some didactic doctrine that might be analyzed by authors of textbooks, but only thanks to the author's ardent, creative, poetic curiosity, which produces, be it in a poem or a prose note, that something "more," that extra je ne sais quoi, as the French say, that is poetry.

For Milosz, it is poetry that generates meaning. If *Roadside Dog* is a soapbox, it is a soapbox for poetry alone (which is served by intelligence and memory). It's true that Milosz's work doesn't lack for doubt, which has its own special niche, but is kept on a chain and not permitted to win in the debate; it is a servant of higher powers. Of course, other forces also come into play. For example, the marvelous sense of humor (which Cioran often lacks) that signals forbearance for the universe's shortcomings and the imperfection of humans (including the author himself).

Poetry and doubt require one another, they coexist like the oak and ivy, like dogs and cats. But their relationship is neither harmonious nor symmetrical. Poetry needs doubt far more than doubt needs poetry. Through doubt, poetry purges itself of rhetorical insincerity, senseless chatter, falsehood, youthful loquacity, empty (inauthentic) euphoria. Released from doubt's stern gaze, poetry—especially in our dark days—might easily degenerate into sentimental ditties, exalted but unthinking song, senseless praise of all the earth's forms.

Things stand differently with doubt: it flees the company of poetry. Poetry is its dread opponent, or more, a fatal threat. Even dark, tragic poetry rises above doubt, annihilates it, annuls its reason for being. Doubt enriches and dramatizes poetry, but poetry liquidates doubt—or at least so dilutes it that the skeptics lose their heads and fall silent, or else become artists.

Doubt is more intelligent than poetry, insofar as it tells malicious tales about the world, things we've long known but struggled to hide from ourselves. But poetry surpasses doubt, pointing to what we cannot know.

Doubt is narcissistic; we look at everything critically, including ourselves, and perhaps that comforts us. Poetry, on the other hand, trusts the world, and rips us from the deep-sea diving suits of our "I"; it believes in the possibility of beauty and its tragedy.

Poetry's argument with doubt has nothing in common with the facile quarrel of optimism and pessimism.

The twentieth century's great drama means that we now deal with two kinds of intellect: the resigned and the seeking, the questing. Doubt is poetry for the resigned. Whereas poetry is searching, endless wandering.

Doubt is a tunnel, poetry is a spiral.

Doubt prefers to shut, while poetry opens.

Poetry laughs and cries, doubt ironizes.

Doubt is death's plenipotentiary, its longest and wittiest shadow; poetry runs toward an unknown goal.

Why does one choose poetry while another chooses doubt? We don't know and we'll never find out. We don't know why one is Cioran and the other is Milosz.

1997

9 Vacation's End

Vacation! What a lovely word! I've come to value its charm all the more since I realized that it didn't mean anything to many of my American friends and acquaintances. The Puritan workaholism that dominates the States doesn't allow for luxuries like real vacations. Why? I've asked my American friends about this many times. The answer I often get is that while we're away on vacation we run the risk of letting our competitors take advantage of our absence. Not directly perhaps, it's not that we'll be fired. But they'll work nonstop through even the summer's worst dog days and get ahead of us in ways we won't be able to undo come winter.

It all reminds me, paradoxically, of the slim books full of Thomistic wisdom written by the German philosopher Josef Pieper, who died not long ago at a truly biblical age. In the 1950s, when an almost Stakhanovite work ethic prevailed in Germany, he perversely and courageously championed the Latin *otium*, that is, serene, aimless, unhurried meditation. Vacation would seem to be both a natural continuation and a crucial modification of *otium*. *Otium* is linked by and large with motion-less study; when I read about *otium*, I think of a room with books, an armchair, and albums of reproductions. Vacation, on the other hand, involves travel (even if only to the summer house where you'll continue your studies). Vacation is travel, and travel is necessarily accompanied by an abundance of minor, annoying indignities. The crucial immobility that resides in the heart of *otium* vanishes the day before you leave; the circling around a suitcase while bearing it various offerings from your closet becomes a parody of vacation mobility. We're still further distanced from *otium*'s stasis by the trip itself, regardless of whether it is undertaken by car, train, horse, or bus.

The journey, or the possibility of one, is not simply a function of material wealth, I should add. The United States is far wealthier than my meager Central European homeland, but when we go to Krakow in August almost all our friends are out of town. There'd be no danger of that in New York. Or almost none.

Returning to the phenomenology of vacations: the trip explodes the serenity of *otium*, it tears us from our favorite books. (Or rather from our choice of bedtime reading—how many books can you take on the road? And who knows if you'll want to keep faith with the authors you picked up while packing?) But the trip, to do it justice, also reveals the limits of this famous *otium*. Staying in your room—the state Pascal praised so highly—can lead at times to sterility, to a specific type of stale, bookish egotism. Books are marvelous company—but the world also merits our attention. On journeys, though, as in dreams, we meet new people and old buildings, we're introduced to places we've never seen. But dreams ordinarily deceive us; dream voices speak too hurriedly, as though fearing the dawn's arrival.

Our little memories can't manage whatever it is that dreams whisper so insistently. Whereas a successful trip takes the shape of an expanded and well-ordered dream. And a prolonged one; even the shortest trip (I'm not counting flying, which has nothing in common with traveling, it's more like short-term hibernation) is slower than a dream, and more comprehensible.

Trips remind us that we read too much, that rich fields of reality spread beyond the library. They summon up the great pleasures of walking, long treks through Italian towns, where we try to stay on the shady side of the street to avoid the ruthless sun. They revive thirst's sweet torment, quenched by a long sip of *acqua senza gas*. In other words, a trip—as long as it's as individualized as possible, not subject to anyone's orders, not restricted by the tour bus driver's suggestions—reawakens the bookworm to his body's presence, its indispensability not just for sports but for art, especially for art. In a certain sense the tiredness we experience during a zealous trip to one of those countries worth visiting echoes the physical exhaustion of the artist-craftsmen who put frescoes into church vaults and wrenched white statues from marble. It also mimics their own mobility and their own arduous journeys from town to town and patron to patron. They relocated, after all, on horse- or donkey-back, or even on foot. (Even in the nineteenth century young artists often covered long distances on foot; you don't often encounter pedestrians today on the road between Warsaw and Krakow.)

During the course of our travels we see people we'd never find in our hometown. At times a local will answer our banal question—"How do I get to such and such a cathedral?"—with such verve that he stays lodged in our memory by way of the charm he imparts to his simple directions: *prima a destra, se-*

conda a sinistra. Even the word *sinistra* loses the ominous ring it has in other languages.

Someone else will sit next to us in a café. We'll exchange a few words with yet another. We should remember that these meetings—if they become true meetings—are a premium, a bonus thrown in by the good spirits of traveling.

Should we travel alone or in company? Opinions are divided. In his essay "Going on a Journey," William Hazlitt insists that traveling be done solo: "I like to go by myself." He quotes Laurence Sterne, who said, "I need a traveling companion in order to observe how the shadows lengthen at sunset." Hazlitt appreciates the poetic quality of Sterne's argument, but doesn't agree, since, so he claims, the constant exchange and comparison of opinions while traveling hinders the spontaneous reactions of the mind, which should remain alone with an alien world.

But my sympathies lie with Sterne for many reasons, not least because on foreign soil you're alone even when you are with someone else. During an Italian *passeggiata* or *corso*, for example, when all the inhabitants of a small town perform their ritual stroll along a precisely prescribed route as if under hypnosis or sleepwalking: new arrivals from distant lands don't register at all, they're completely invisible. The tourist has so little reality that traveling with at least one companion fortifies us, braces us a bit. Of course, this company must be carefully selected. Wasn't it Samuel Johnson who said that the pleasantest thing was to find oneself in a coach with a pretty, intelligent woman?

We admired one such *passeggiata* this year on the streets of Lucca: the elderly, the middle-aged, young mothers proudly pushing baby carriages, groups of girls in their best T-shirts and crowds of laughing boys pretending not to notice, peeking slyly at one another. Such varied generations strolling beside one another through the evening streets seems at times like a bizarre metaphysical joke. It's as if time were mocking us, showing us human destiny, or rather, one human fate presented simultaneously (or synchronically, as a half-baked structuralist might say), magnified, multiplied many times over. If so, then the infant, the teenager, the sober middle-aged father, and the grandfather perched on a brick wall would all be one person, the same inhabitant of Lucca! Likewise all the women, from the little girl to the gray-haired, garrulous old lady, would be merely the multiplication of a single woman.

One inconvenience of nearly every trip, however, is that it strips us of music. You can't count on concerts waiting at every stop along the road; and the many summer music festivals may not prove particularly enticing. Their audiences aren't made up of travelers, moreover, but of those who stay in one place. But anyone who wants to experience the pleasures of a renewed acquaintance with music come September will agree to a few weeks of fasting. You may even be better off not bringing along one or another portable player—there are so many nowadays— so as to experience a true musical famine, unsated by pale imitations.

Lucca. Muratov described it as poor, provincial, and neglected back at the turn of the century, but it's a prosperous, seemingly complacent town today. Its famous fortifications, which haven't had anything to fend off for ages, serve locals and tourists alike as a splendid park and walkway both around and beyond the town; you come across bicyclists, strolling couples, local joggers, and American students gazing at Italy with eyes wide open. The good fortune of Lucca, which has apparently profited both from tourism and from Italy's economic miracle, seems so great that we mistrust our own senses when we spot the prison—gloomy and gray like all prisons, illuminated with trembling neon light—from the fortications one evening. How can happy Lucca, which was governed, apparently quite well, for several years by Elisa Bonaparte, the usurper's sister, have a prison? But it does.

Lucca doesn't differ much from other Tuscan towns. But if you stay on a bit longer, carefully observing its homes and churches, you'll discover—yet again!—the manifest, remarkable Italian talent for architectural detail, that frantic gift for shaping little piazzas, decorating walls, erecting glorious churches.

Lucca holds one particularly distinctive square—the Piazza dell' Anfiteatro—which retains the exact shape of a Roman amphitheater. This must be one of the most unusual ways ever used to preserve the past—the amphitheater is no longer there, but the square serves as its negative, its imprint. The small stones with concave frontals covered in pastel plaster evoke the Romans' presence. This oval expanse was uncovered only in the nineteenth century; earlier it had been overgrown with hovels, and before that, centuries ago, the amphitheater's Roman marble had been stripped by local builders who used it to construct Lucca's churches. Its shrines thus arose in some sense from the weather-beaten sporting passions of the ancient Romans. Today, though, this square good-humoredly reconciles everyday Italian life with the onslaught of tourists; motley laundry dries on the balconies while a tired tourist from Arizona naps in the café garden. One balcony in particular, the highest, crowns the amphitheater's western pole and reigns over the square: a mass of gorgeous flowers spills from it.

Lucca gives the impression of being homogeneous; the ancient fortifications that frame it reinforce the sense that a fragment of the distant past has been miraculously preserved. But our strolls through the old town, especially on July afternoons, took place in a vacuum (only at dusk did the streets come to life). The town's inhabitants seemed to have fled. They'd left, no doubt, for the nearby beaches—Lucca isn't far from the famous seaside resorts of Livorno, where the poet Slowacki sat out his quarantine, Viareggio, or Forte dei Marmi. So the northern visitors were tempted by the seaside too. Sightseeing one day, swimming the next, we decided. Not in Viareggio, though, or Forte dei Marmi, where thin, dreary beaches preside over water so shallow that it seems more like the Dead Sea than the Mediterranean, a bit further, beyond the border dividing Tuscany from Liguria, in Bocca di Magra, a small town set in a somewhat different landscape.

The road to Bocca leads along the coast and calls to mind a corridor in a very long apartment, a corridor crossed every moment by someone in slippers, a damp towel, and dripping hair. Young people on the ubiquitous scooters and motorbikes, as if transposed from an Italian neorealist film, hurriedly surmount the distance from beach to home, home to beach. All these never-ending beaches are thronged, besieged, as if the Italian population counted some two billion. A sign for "Shelley's Restaurant" juts out beside the highway—a reminder that the nearby town of Lerici holds the last home of the English poet, who drowned when a storm flooded his sailboat. (Unlike Byron, Shelley couldn't swim; to this day poets are divided into those who swim and those who stay out of the water.)

From the road, you can also see the white mountains above Carrara, what's left of the marble from the famous quarries of antiquity. We see these same white mountains later, while we're swimming; they adorn the horizon like fake tropical glaciers, partly screened from time to time by a rippling curtain of heat. In Bocca di Magra there are far fewer vacationers than along the smoother shores; Bocca's coastline is rocky and the devotees of all-day tanning at the beach (which is something like the summertime equivalent to hours spent staring at the television screen) undoubtably revolt at the thought of a rocky bed along this stony shore.

Bocca di Magra (the mouth of the river Magra, which flows down from the nearest mountains, the Apennines) is a historical spot in a different sense. Mary McCarthy vacationed here. The Polish reader of Czeslaw Milosz's work will also remember this town. Nicola Chiaromonte used to come here, as did Hannah Arendt. These venerable shades bathed here, in this same warm, velvety, deep green water. Mr. Milosz, who has nothing of the shade about him, still recalls perfectly the charm of those by-gone vacations, the motorboat trips to Punta Bianca (motorboats still transport eager fugitives from the smooth beaches) and swimming in the ocean.

You can also reach Punta Bianca by way of a steep path, pausing to rest on the roof of the German bunker that adorns even this picturesque promontory. It's apparently difficult to dispose of Hitler's bunkers; built, like our Soviet housing blocks, of reinforced concrete, they resist time's incursions. Unfortunately, ugliness sometimes dreams of eternity too. Who knows, maybe a thousand years from now, fathers will smilingly point them out to their children (in which case the goal of building a thousand-year Reich of sorts will be—ironically—fulfilled). Let's hope they won't be confused with the traces of ancient Greece and Rome.

But maybe Bocca di Magra has simply fallen out of fashion? It's a fairly substantive doubt, linked as it is with the tricky problem of vacationing multitudes. How do you survive a European vacation in July or August, when half the continent, in consort with an army of bold Dutchmen towing their trailers along every highway, finds itself in motion? What's more, we ourselves, for all our aristocratic pretenses, also form part of this horde. What is to be done? There's no easy answer to the question so beloved of the Russian radical intelligentsia. To avoid the beaten track may be the only solution. Sometimes it's simple; in Prague you need only detour slightly from the main tourist trail to find yourself on an empty street. Sometimes it's more difficult; Lucca is small and holds almost no sidetracks or margins.

We sidestepped the main track once by visiting a new museum in seaside La Spezia. The museum, the Museo Amedeo Lia, opened in December of 1996. A successful engineer, Mr. Lia himself provided the funding. Since it's not yet in the popular guidebooks by means of which tourists (us included, I won't hide it) hop across Europe like blind men with canes, it was virtually empty. The museum occupies a meticulously restored Franciscan monastery and is ultramodern, even air-conditioned, which isn't always the case in Italy. But its real distinction lies in its marvelously displayed exhibits, particularly the old paintings, which are placed on large light gray boards. Many museums have a fatal proclivity for cramming early paintings into a tiny space, apparently guided by the principle that since these artists weren't yet familiar with individualist pride they should be displayed in large squadrons. The pictures here avoid that fate.

I don't know of any other museum that provides such splendid conditions for studying the paintings of the trecento and quattrocento. The two large halls in which they're grouped give the impression of an endless holiday; even the museum guards are cheerful, not bored in the least. This attests to the gallery's success. Every painting draws our attention and the light back-drop permits us to do justice to the miraculous, fresh colors.

The engineer Amedeo Lia is a very elderly gentleman today, we discover from a text in the museum; he had, and still has, excellent taste. A number of early paintings are fixed in our memory, Lippo di Benivieni's *Descent from the Cross*, Paolo di Giovanni Fei's *Annunciation*, and several others. Of the later work, we'll perhaps single out chiefly Pontormo's marvelous *Self-Portrait* (with a question mark attached—is it really him?), painted, it would seem, at the same time as van Gogh's self-portraits: the gaze of a young artist which contains both fear and aplomb, not an uncommon combination.

One work stands out among the sculptures, the exceptional fifteenth-century head by Francesco Laurana. It's sculpted in clay; two cracks running across the forehead make it look like a skull. It's not a skull, though, but a head with a kind, intelligent face and closed eyes. Francesco Laurana's head looks fragile somehow, as though it has been traveling alone somewhere in space. Marble heads are different, they share their material's majesty; this clay shell, on the other hand, holds both life and death (and sleep), like each of us.

Our vacation was scarred by news of Zbigniew Herbert's death. By chance, we learned of it in Italy, in his favorite country (let's turn for a moment to the anthem's words, "from the Polish land to Italy . . ."). The Swedish translator Anders Bodegard called us with the news from Stockholm (he'd visited us a few days earlier in Lucca). As a high school student in Gliwice I read *Barbarian in the Garden*; at the time, in my Silesian high school, it was difficult for me to believe in the splendors of Siena and Tuscany, which seemed more exotic than Martian canals. Now I no longer doubted . . .

Herbert's poems and essays taught us many things, not just courage and intelligence but also how to look at paintings and ancient towns. It's also true, of course, that what was greatest in them eludes such utilitarian formulations. What does the phrase "taught us" mean, since the essence of his poetry and essays was something completely disinterested, great joy, great sorrow, at times mourning, shivers of rapture, the need for fidelity, the praise of wisdom. He had perfect pitch. I imagined him sometimes in the white apron of a conservator of antiquities, standing, pen and brush in hand, with a worried face and a playful smile in a vast sunlit hall filled with statues, trees, and people. What he conserved, though, was not works of art but the world as such. Obviously, he was not a conservative; this category doesn't exist in great poetry. He was a splendid magician; the stones of Siena still miss him.

10 Should We Visit Sacred Places?

There's no point in visiting mythological sites, I thought. It's not worth traveling to cities whose weight in our memory is as ponderous as a bronze monument. We shouldn't do it simply because we won't be able to cope with the experience, the intense emotion. Lvov has been for many years the single real place, the single image of the world for my father, who was born and raised there. He systematically refuses all opportunities to visit, though. I was born in Lvov, but left before really seeing it. Recently, however, I returned from a trip to Ukraine and showed my father my freshly developed photos; he instantly recognized and identified every street, every alley, virtually every building—after fifty-six years!

Like a thriving tailor's shop, our spiritual life relies on hiring a fair number of assistants, cutters, and seamstresses, whose tasks are not simply separate but mutually contradictory. The calm, perhaps slightly melancholy helpers maintain myths in a state of virginal purity, shielding them from scholars' eyes. The others, busy skeptics, wield their enormous scissors as they endlessly revise and shamelessly criticize the same myths.

The invitation sent out by Heinrich-Böll-Stiftung, the foundation that organized an international conference in Lvov in 2001, apparently fell into the hands of this second type—not the guardians of myth but its opponents—who must have rubbed their palms in glee, repeating, "Yes, of course, let him go, maybe that will finally cure his love for this obscure little city on the outskirts of Europe."

We arrived in Lvov late at night, in the atmosphere of unreal coziness created by every comfortable bus, a fortress of warm security and sleepiness, a mobile monument of civilization from which the representatives of a better world peer out at an imperfect reality. This impression was reinforced by the hideous post-communist apartment blocks that took hazy shape outside the window, the same kind of building that rises everywhere from Kamchatka to Lipski, menhirs adorning the Soviet empire's ruins—but these were somehow sadder. (A technically, if not philosophically, improved edition of these structures can also be seen everywhere from Leipzig to Lisbon.)

For all that, sometime before eight on Thursday the twenty-fourth of May, I opened the curtains of my hotel room on the sixth floor overlooking the deep green Jesuit Garden where one of my nineteenth-century cousins, a lawyer and poet, caught such a bad cold that he died soon after of pneumonia and ever since has been reduced to an elegant shadow in an oil portrait. And I was greeted by a dazzling view of a beautiful city, bright gold in the sharp sunlight. My little flock of inner mockers fell silent, their scissors frozen. For all three days of my stay in Lvov the sun was absolute master of the sky. I saw before me a calm, golden city which I viewed from a double elevation; the Jesuit Garden itself ascends a hill, and the six floors of my hotel rose on top of this (the hotel was new, built sometime in the eighties). I saw church spires in the distance—I could make out the cathedral tower, the Dominican church's green cupola, and the town hall tower, and I guessed where the Bernardines' ornate façade must be. I knew where the main square was, I imagined the theater, hidden in the lower levels of this early morning jungle, I picked out the hill of the High Castle, shutting out the view like a movie screen—and further, to the right, still framed by the city woods, was Kajzerwald, the district in which rose the little house bought by my grandfather in the twenties, the house where I was born.

I had before me a city that was both absolutely foreign and completely familiar, forgotten, forsaken, surrendered, mourned, bullet-ridden, but still truly existing, vividly and persuasively illuminated, solid, living, a city in which I could immediately make out the most important churches, whose general topography held no secrets for me, spread wide in the flatlands, tucked between hills, serene, stately. You shouldn't visit mythic places, there's no way to see them, catch them, seize them. They're easy to recognize, but what then? What's to be done? After a long moment, I capitulated and reached for my Japanese camera in order to eternalize the city's astonishing, early morning performance. I took a picture that I view unmoved today, that retains almost nothing, the May gleam has lost its glory, the towers can scarcely be seen, only the trees' leaves flaunt their easy universalism and a television transmitter tower juts through the morning mist.

Fortunately I didn't have to decide anything, I could save my questions and indecisions for later. The first day was devoted entirely to learned political and economic disquisitions: the problem of the present-day Ukrainian-Polish border was discussed with an eye to Poland's future membership in the European

Union. I admired the knowledge and eloquence of my colleagues, who remembered the dates of every pogrom, uprising, and international conference; this may sound glib, but I mean it. I also liked the passion with which they addressed the question of the future. I listened with great sympathy to the local participants, who openly spoke of the troubles of present-day Ukrainian life and looked with hope and envy to their western neighbor, Poland. They were also critical of Poland, particularly the participants representing Poland's Ukrainian minority. I compromised myself, though, when I was unexpectedly called upon to respond. (I was supposed to summarize the evolution of Polish historians' attitudes toward the Ukrainian problem in the 1970s and 1980s!) I let everyone down completely, thus confirming the negative opinion that reasonable people everywhere have entertained toward poets for the last three thousand years or so.

The next day, after having aired their pessimistic predictions on Ukraine's future and the possibility of her membership in the European Union, the other conference guests packed their bags and headed back to Germany and Poland chiefly, or perhaps they sped off to the next international conference on Europe's urgent worries. But I had just begun my pilgrim's project, with its hazy prerogatives and obligations. I found myself, after all, in what was for me the most extraordinary spot on earth, in my city, which wasn't mine, about which I knew next to nothing, in a foreign city, about which I knew a good deal, which was finally just a bit mine. It was as if the beautiful definition *docta ignorantia* had abandoned the books' pages to become a living wound on Europe's green map. But what was I supposed to do? How does a pilgrim from such a strange sect behave? There are, after all, no guidebooks for ignorant people born in Lvov. There are no instructions for people like me, who spent only four months in Lvov and know nothing—a Japanese camera can't capture time past, a prewar city map says nothing of the present.

Propelled by a sense of obligation, the next morning I set out for the art gallery directly across from the former Ossolineum and looked at dozens of French and Italian paintings, darkened canvases hanging on long-unpainted walls. It was clear that the museum had no money—like a number of Polish museums. I also saw a fair amount of Polish painting from the late nineteenth and early twentieth centuries.

By going to the art gallery, I was acting just as I would in an Italian or French town: like a tourist. I felt the whole time, though, that this wasn't the proper way to behave in this town.

Someone who respects myth and remembrance, as I did in Lvov, is plunged into something like a narcissistic reverie. He thus seeks out dark and empty places, museum halls or shady parks. He feels ill at ease, though, on streets radiant with May sunshine, especially when viewing the Ukrainian crowds filling the bright streets. This crowd, sometimes young and carefree, other times old and careworn, poor, sometimes dressed in peasant, not urban, fashion, shatters the reveries, disrupts the speculations. A sui generis situation: to be in a city that is, in Mandelstam's phrase, "familiar to tears, to the veins, to the child's swollen glands," on the one hand, but filled with entirely different, foreign crowds. Not even different from those I knew, since I can't claim to have known Lvov's prewar crowds, but different from Krakow's or Warsaw's or even Gliwice's crowds. Plunged into dreams, I walked along the street, drowning in the brilliant sun. I checked street names on the prewar city map my father sent me, without taking the new, Ukrainian onomastics too seriously. German tourists must stroll through Gdansk or Wroclaw the same way, absorbed in dreams, ignoring the present-day city. Young Israelis or Jewish Americans must likewise walk the streets of Krakow's Jewish district, Kazimierz, seeking traces of the prewar life, sunk in reverie. We're like ghosts, impatiently driving the present, the new life, away. Since the new life in old cities strikes us as imperfect, accidental, provisional, and finally superfluous.

In some sense all these dreamers seeking the past—to whom I belonged for the three days I spent walking Lvov's streets and parks—are the ideal conservatives, they replicate perfectly conservatives' impotence. They search for something that doesn't exist, something that may never have existed, insofar as they beautify the urban crowd whose chimera they chase. They seek better, more beautiful times, and even if some obliging shaman agreed to resurrect what they desire for five minutes, that is, life before the disaster, the crowds, the clouds, the window displays, the shrubs before the disaster, they would still cry out in dismay, "Oh no, that's not it, it was far more marvelous before!"

My magician—a different, wiser magician—turned up in the person of Andrij Pawlyszyn, a young Ukrainian, an editor of the journal *Ji*, well known in Lvov, with perfect Polish and a good working knowledge of Polish literature. He offered to show me the city and did in fact spend half a day walking through Lvov with me. He picked a roundabout route leading through Lyczakow and the High Castle to the neighborhood of the main square. On Akademicka (that's the prewar street name, but he also knew the old names) he pointed out the spot where the local philosophers used to gather in the café Szkocka. A moment later we passed a group of young people speaking Russian. Andrij said these must be the students from the Polish school who always chat in Russian on the street. His knowledge helped me return to earth. We saw the building at 55 Lyczakowska Street where Zbigniew Herbert had lived. Andrij told me about the efforts to have a plaque put up. We also went down Piaskowa Street—a few steps from Lyczakowska—to see the house that had once belonged to my grandfather. If I'd been on my own, I would have been happy just to look at the lattice, the wicket, the rusty doorknob and the tree in the garden. I might not even have remembered that the property visible from the street in fact belonged to someone else, and that my old family home stood hidden behind the front building. I would, in other words, have committed an error typical of those ghosts who stroll through new cities following the directions in an old guidebook, ghosts so ethereal that they sometimes go into raptures over the wrong address. But Andrij suggested that we visit the old house; he rang the doorbell and explained through the intercom who we were and what we were doing. After a long pause an elderly lady, suspicious at first but then very friendly, let us into the garden and then the house itself.

Thus I saw for the first time the legendary family house from within; it was occupied now by the old lady and her dermatologist son. And all this was thanks to my guide. (I had been in Lvov once before, when I was a student, but I hadn't dared then to knock at the door of my ex-home.)

I then understood the importance of such a guide—intelligent and well versed in the various new layers of reality without discounting the past. A guide who saves us from misty mysticism.

Yes, I thought sitting in the airplane, we should visit mythic places, even if it means sorrow and hard moments. We should visit mythic places because they are the axis, the pole of our life, jutting into frosty ether. We must visit them, but only if accompanied by a sober, trustworthy guide.

At the little Lvov airport four sandstone socialist realist sculptures bade me farewell—a soldier, a peasant woman, a pilot, and a worker. They stood at attention in the bright May sun like heroes of a forgotten Greek epic.

11 Intellectual Krakow

The structure of many European (and North American) cities is governed by a mysterious law, which I have discovered and which may one day bear my name. Districts on the east side of town are generally proletariat in character, while western districts are bourgeois and comparatively intellectual. Just take a look at maps of London, Paris, Berlin, to name but a few metropolises. Aren't I right? The same pattern turns up time and again. In London we have, as everyone knows, the East and West Ends. In Paris, the wealthy sixteenth district is on the west, while the humbler twelfth and twentieth districts lie eastward. The western suburbs are likewise safer and more prosperous than their eastern counterparts. West Berlin was the wealthy part of town long before the wall went up. This law also holds for Warsaw.

I've spoken with knowledgeable geographers and sociologists who've been unable to explain this phenomenon. Does this peculiarity of city planning perhaps reflect the medieval principle of building churches along an east-west axis?

Krakow—a far smaller town than the behemoths I've mentioned—is subject to the same principle. The bourgeoisie and intellectuals have long since divided the territory west of the Market Square between them. Under communist rule this region grew grayer and became the kind of district that traditional guidebooks would be hard pressed to define. For Krakow's inhabitants, who don't require guidebooks, the answer was and remains simply "the intellectual district."

West of Market Square: that is, up Szewska Street past the Planty Gardens to Karmelicka Street and then Krolewska, and then along both sides of this axis, up to Wola Justowska. The intellectuals' apartments hid, and still hide, along both sides of Karmelicka Street in the quiet buildings on the side streets. The editor Jerzy Turowicz, who ran the Catholic newspaper *Tygodnik Powszechny* wisely and courageously for over fifty years, lived here until his death. The novelist and essayist Hanna Malewska lived here. Andrzej Kijowski was born here. The philosopher Roman Ingarden lived a bit further down. As did the historian Henryk Wereszycki. The composer Wladyslaw Zelenski lived here before then. And there were many others. And who didn't live in the Writers' House on Krupnicza Street at one time or another? That's where the painter and writer Stanislaw Wyspianski was born as well. The splendid painters Jozef Mehoffer and Wojciech Weiss also lived on Krupnicza. The Rostworowski family lived nearby on Salwator.

Exceptions do occur: the president of Polish poetry, and Polish intellectuals, Czeslaw Milosz lives not far from Market Square, but on the southeast side. The poet Ryszard Krynicki and his wife, the publisher Krystyna Krynicka, live even further off, across the Vistula River in Podgorze.

But let's get back to the western territories: all these remark-

able sites were left in ruins, or at least an advanced state of neglect, following the Nazi and Stalinist years.

This is why, seen with a cold, objective eye, these homes
and streets don't seem to conceal any mystery. When my friend
the American poet Edward Hirsch came to Krakow in the fall of
1996 to interview Wislawa Szymborska for *The New York Times*
Magazine—she'd just received the Nobel Prize—he called the
area she lived in then (on Chocimska Street) "proletarian and
nondescript."

Nondescript. I was outraged and objected: I tried to explain
that he hadn't discerned the streets' latent nobility, the delicate
gleam of certain windows, the charm of their small parks, the
possibilities contained by certain courtyards.

I realized then that someone like myself who loves Krakow
and has known it for years must perfect a complex system of
perceptions. In other words, I understood that I saw the possibilities, the potentialities, the unfulfilled entelechies of this district, I sensed what it might become under more favorable
conditions. I knew how many truly great artists had lived here
(Wislawa Szymborska's neighbors for many years included the
writer Kornel Filipowicz and the director Tadeusz Kantor; the director Krystian Lupa apparently still lives somewhere nearby).
And I had mentally mixed their talents with the houses' unprepossessing plaster. I also knew the district's past, I was familiar
with its history and could imagine its bygone charms. At the
same time few of its homes could match such expectations
today. Even the famous "professors'" house at the corner of
Slowacki Boulevard and Lobzowska Street, where university em-
ployees once lived—it was nicknamed the "coffin" due to its
black ceramic façade—now blended into its banal surroundings.

My American friend had seen only what really existed; a

run-down district with lopsided sidewalks, streets full of pot-holes, buildings needing new plaster with drunks huddled in their doorways. Whereas I saw neighborhoods that had given birth to books, paintings, plays, and performances. I also sometimes knew, or imagined with the help of books and the tales of older cousins, what these buildings and gardens had once been, and what they had held. But a new arrival from another, sober, empirical world could perceive only shabby, tired objects.

The venerable, medieval, Renaissance, or baroque Krakow is a different matter: the massive forms of churches and palaces don't need desperate feats of imagination, they're clearly defined against the sky's backdrop both day and evening, as the sun slowly descends. But the intellectual district demands a different approach. Only visitors from other ex-communist countries can truly understand this, since they've witnessed the same process—the fading of cities. They still remember that certain cities, or perhaps just certain districts, can best be caught by way of sympathetic imagination, aided by a rudimentary knowledge of history: such spots escape the camera's objective eye.

Later I thought that perhaps my mistake, my optimistic vision of the district and my reaction to my American friend's incomprehension, might be something more than an accidental optical or psychological phenomenon.

Perhaps we view not only certain districts but even our country as such too leniently, expanding reality through reverie, enhancing a sometimes dreary external world by means of introspection.

Perhaps that's why we have poetry.

12 Gray Paris

Paris, photographed through thousands of lenses (Japanese tourists experiencing a moment of mechanized eternity on every bridge), consumed daily by the greedy gazes of the photographic devices deployed by tourists from various continents, has not ceased to exist . . . It lives on, endlessly resisting the onslaught of gazes. There's the lighthearted Paris of song, the Paris of romantic snapshots: the stairs of Montmartre, the setting sun's rays on the Pont Neuf, the autumn leaves in the Luxembourg Garden, the frivolous Paris of films. But there's also another Paris.

All who've come to this city by way of Europe's (or America's) provinces remember the first album of Parisian photos we viewed at a friend's or flipped through with a mixture of rapture and disdain while visiting some aunt or uncle: rooftops on the Ile Saint-Louis, the church of Saint-Germain (the Romanesque style blended in this name with recollections of some Gothic Juliette Greco), a gentle wave on the gray Seine.

We leafed through this album with a touch of scorn, since

the longing to visit this mythical city was mixed with a vivid sense that these photographs, intended precisely for us provincials, were in fact classic tourist kitsch. I don't know why, but autumn always prevailed in those delicate, pastel pictures, as if the albums' editors knew that November's sweet warmth best captures France's capital.

The best-known city in Europe . . . So well known that newcomers from other countries, nourished on movies, postcards, and those autumnal albums above which rises a slim, anorexic Eiffel Tower, scarcely feel any surprise: we know it, we know this place, they cry. We know that tower, the Parisian rooftops, the clipped boughs of the plane trees, the little trapezoidal squares on which two Paulownia trees grow. We know the café gardens and the little homes nestled up against Haussmann's showy structures. We know the metro line where, on wintry afternoons, you can stare directly into strangers' apartments—and the imperial façades of Napoleonic edifices.

To photograph Paris—after all this! After painters, sketchers, photographers, after memoirists and writers! After Walter Benjamin and Paul Léautaud! Is it possible?

Apparently so. You just have to try—and to possess a "point of view," not talent and a good camera alone.

I have before me the photographs of Bogdan Konopka, depicting a Paris I know well. At first glance, though, I can't seem to get my bearings—I don't know these houses, these courtyards, I don't know this derelict railway or this park sprinkled with snow. Where is the Place de la Concorde, the Boulevard Saint-Germain, where's my favorite bookshop, where's the garden of the Palais Royal with its young lindens? They're not here, I see only anemic little streets, flimsy houses, unprepossessing stairwells. Above all, I don't find the splendid Parisian light, the refulgence with which the oceanic Atlantic climate repays Paris for the rain, the towering cumuli, the cold and damp it provides all winter, spring and fall. Bogdan Konopka's photographs show a faded city; paradoxically they too have something autumnal about them, like the more conventional albums I've mentioned. Here, though, the mute, matte still lifes of streets take the place of golden leaves and subtle shadows: this is actual, aggravating November.

I can perfectly imagine the outrage of Paris's admirers, be they French or foreign. Where's the light? Where the Pont des Arts? I can hear the angry voices: this photographer's driven by malice. He's come from some small, dark country, maybe even a small, dark town in a small, dark country, and wants to strip Paris of its majestic light, its bright sandstone columns, its freshly scrubbed Panthéon, its beautiful broad streets, the new pyramid in the Louvre's courtyard, its splendid museums.

Does the perpetrator of these photographs thus require a defense? And what shape might this *plaidoyer* take?

I see several lines of potential defense. First, the counsel for the defense might appeal to the dominant aesthetic of today's photography, its muted mood, as well as the distinctive "turpism"—that is, an infatuation with "ugliness" in both subject matter and its formal presentation—that seems to typify the work of contemporary art photographers. And certainly the chief motive is resistance to commercial photography: photography's beauty has been hijacked, abducted by the cunning craftsmen of the camera, fashion photographers, the creators of the covers for popular women's magazines. They don't lack for beauty: every page of *Elle* or *Vogue* proudly displays lovely photographs of lovely girls, lovely homes, lovely spring meadows above which lovely birds glide.

The counsel for the defense might take into consideration the age's aesthetics. And this wouldn't be to the detriment of Konopka's work. Acknowledging the norms of his own historical moment doesn't discredit him in the least.

But the defense must go further. It must prove that something else is at stake here. Bogdan Konopka does this remarkable city a service by showing us another Paris, the Paris of courtyards and gray stairwells, the Paris of gloomy afternoons. By evoking the secret fraternity of all cities, beautiful and ugly, he liberates Paris from the isolation into which it has been thrust by its own eminence, its unique status among the European capitals. Since how can one live a normal life, die a normal death in a Paris shown only from its finest, most glittering angle, displayed only in its most "imperial," elegant, ministerial light?

Anyone who's ever driven across the Czech Republic, Poland, or eastern Germany has no doubt seen boundlessly sad, gray towns and cities. Clearly Paris shares nothing in common with them, it's totally different—and yet, Konopka tells us in his photographs' calm voice, take a closer look at certain Parisian neighborhoods, streets, courtyards. And you'll perceive in them, as in an ancient mosaic, fragments of Mikolow and Pilsen, chips of Myslenice and East Berlin. This won't be lèse-majesté, it's not attempted assassination; no, it's rather an effort to find what the great metropolis shares with a modest town on Europe's peripheries. It's an attempt to cast a bridge between the meek, the mundane, and imperial glory.

While looking at these photographs, I also noticed that there's not a single scrap of the Paris erected by Baron Haussmann's titanic efforts. (I should confess that this Paris annoys me at times with its bourgeois regularity, the solidity of the buildings designed to house the Notary, the Physician, the Engineer, the Lawyer, the Pharmacist and the Dentist.) We're dealing here with the pre- and post-Haussmann Paris, a city still containing traces of organic medieval construction (as in the surviving islets of old Paris) as well as modernity's chaos.

Finally—as Konopka's defense lawyer might conclude—the grayness of this Paris may reflect a certain disillusionment that is difficult, even shameful, to express, the disillusionment so well described by Czeslaw Milosz. Of course people are still enchanted by what is truly enchanting, and they still go on pilgrimage to Paris. But they also sense a certain lack. The city still exists, of course, it stands, washed by André Malraux, enhanced by new museums and monumental structures, but the great light of intellect that once reigned here, that drew young writers and artists from throughout the world—Jerzy Stempowski speaks mournfully of a Central Laboratory that has closed up shop—has dimmed, faded, and even the eyes of cameras accustomed to registering other parameters, more physical in nature, can't help noticing. Bogdan Konopka took pictures of Paris, not its myth.

13 Young Poets, Please Read Everything

I sense at least one danger here. By discussing ways of reading, or simply sketching a portrait of a "good reader," I may inadvertently give the impression that I am myself a perfect reader. Nothing could be further from the truth. I'm a chaotic reader, and the holes in my education are more breathtaking than the Swiss Alps. My remarks should thus be seen as belonging to the realm of dreams, a kind of a personal utopia, rather than as describing one of my very small platoon of virtues.

Reading chaotically! Some time ago I unpacked the suitcase from my summer vacation. Let's take a look at the books I took with me to Switzerland, near Lake Geneva. I probably should have brought Jean-Jacques Rousseau, Byron, Madame de Staël, Juliusz Slowacki, Adam Mickiewicz, Gibbon, and Nabokov, since all of these are linked with this renowned lake in one way or another. But none of them actually made the trip with me. I see on my study's floor instead Jacob Burckhardt's *The Greeks and Greek Civilization* (yes, in English translation, I picked it up in a Houston half-price bookstore); a selection of Emerson's essays, Baudelaire's poetry in French, Stefan George's poems in Polish translation, Hans Jonas's classic book on Gnosticism (in German), some of Zbigniew Herbert's poems, and the volume of Hugo von Hofmannsthal's voluminous *Collected Works* (*Gesammelte Werke*) containing his remarkable essays. Some of these books belong to various Parisian libraries. This suggests that I'm a rather neurotic reader who often shuns an owner's responsibilities in favor of library books, as if reading books that don't belong to me grants me some additional measure of freedom (libraries—the only venue in which the socialist project has succeeded).

But why do I read? Do I really need to answer this question? It seems to me that poets read for all kinds of reasons, some of which are quite straightforward and don't differ from the motives of any other mortal. But our reading takes place chiefly beneath two signs: the sign of memory and the sign of ecstasy. We read for memory (for knowledge, education) because we are curious about what our many precursors produced before our own minds were opened. This is what we call tradition—or history.

We also read for ecstasy. Why? Just because. Because books contain not only wisdom and well-ordered information but also a kind of energy that comes close to dance and shamanistic drunkenness. This is especially true of (some) poetry. Because we ourselves experience those strange moments when we are driven by a force that demands strict obedience and sometimes, though not always, leaves behind black spots on paper the way a fire leaves ashes (*noircir le papier*, as the French call the noble act of writing). And once you've undergone a moment of ecstatic writing, you start acting like a drug addict who always craves more. You'd do anything for more of it; and reading doesn't seem like an excessive sacrifice.

The books I read—if any such confession is required or desired—fall into these two categories, books of memory and of ecstasy. You can't read an ecstatic book late at night: insomnia ensues. You read history before falling asleep, and save Rimbaud for noon. The relationship between memory and ecstasy is rich, paradoxical, and engaging. Sometimes ecstasy grows from memory, and then spreads like a forest fire—an old sonnet seized by a greedy eye may ignite the spark of a new poem. But memory and ecstasy do not always overlap. Sometimes a sea of indifference divides them.

There are scholars whose memory is astonishingly vast and yet they produce very little. Sometimes in the library you catch sight of an old man wearing a bow tie, bent beneath the weight of years, and you think: That person knows everything. And some of these elderly readers in thick glasses do indeed know a great deal (though perhaps not that little old man you glimpsed the other day). But this is leagues apart from creativity. At the other end of the spectrum we have the teenagers getting high on hip-hop, but we don't expect to reap a rich artistic harvest from this particular passion.

Apparently memory and ecstasy need each other desperately. Ecstasy requires a little knowledge and memory loses nothing when colored by strong emotions. The problem of reading is so vital for us—us meaning poets, but also just people who like to think, to meditate—because our education has been so imperfect. The liberal schools you attended (or the communist schools where I studied) cared very little for the classics, and were even less interested in the giants of modernity. Our schools are proud of producing streamlined members of that Great Animal, the new society of proud consumers. It's true that we weren't tortured like adolescents in nineteenth-century England (or France or Germany, or even Poland for that matter): we didn't have to memorize the whole of Virgil and Ovid. We must be self-taught; the difference in this regard between someone like Joseph Brodsky, who left school at the age of fifteen and proceeded to read everything he could get his hands on, and someone who's successfully run the full gamut of a modern American education, including a Ph.D., while rarely setting foot outside the Ivy League's safe precincts, doesn't require much comment. We do our reading mainly off-campus and in our post-campus lives. The American poets I know are very well read and yet I see clearly that they have acquired their knowledge in the interval between graduating and entering the zone of middle age. Most American graduate students know rather little, less than their European counterparts, but many of them will make up for this in the years to come.

I also have the impression that many younger American poets read rather narrowly today; they chiefly read poetry and not much else except perhaps a little criticism. To be sure, there's nothing wrong with reading poetry from Homer to Zbigniew Herbert and Anne Carson, and yet it seems to me that this mode of reading is too specialized. It's like having a student of biology tell you: I read only biology. Or a young astronomer who reads only astronomy. Or an athlete reading only the sports section of *The New York Times*. There's nothing terribly wrong with reading "only" poetry—and yet a shadow of premature professionalization hovers over this practice. A shadow of shallowness.

Reading "only" poetry suggests that there's something rigid and isolated about the nature of contemporary poetic practice, that poetry has become separated from philosophy's central questions, from the historian's anxieties, the painter's quandaries, the qualms of an honest politician, e.g., from the deep, common source of culture. The way a young poet organizes his reading is actually quite crucial for the place of poetry among other arts. It may determine—and not only for a single individual—whether poetry is a central discipline (even if read solely by the happy few), responding to the key impulses of a given historic moment, or a more or less interesting form of drudgery that for some reason continues to draw a few unhappy fans.

Or perhaps it's the other way around. Our patterns of reading reflect our deeper, perhaps not entirely conscious, conclusions on the central—or peripheral—place of poetry. Are we satisfied with the specialist's timid approach, with the cautious, sectarian relationship to literature typical of those writers who agree to confine themselves to little tales of broken hearts? Or will we aspire rather to the generous stance of the poet who struggles to think, to sing, to take risks, to embrace generously and boldly the thinning humanity of our time (without forgetting the broken hearts)? So, young poets, please read everything, read Plato and Ortega y Gasset, Horace and Hölderlin, Ronsard and Pascal, Dostoevsky and Tolstoy, Oscar Milosz and Czeslaw Milosz, Keats and Wittgenstein, Emerson and Emily Dickinson, T. S. Eliot and Umberto Saba, Thucydides and Colette, Apollinaire and Virginia Woolf, Anna Akhmatova and Dante, Pasternak and Machado, Montaigne and St. Augustine, Proust and Hofmannsthal, Sappho and Szymborska, Thomas Mann and Aeschylus, read biographies and treatises, essays and political analyses. Read for yourselves, read for the sake of your inspiration, for the sweet turmoil in your lovely head. But also read against yourselves, read for questioning and impotence, for despair and erudition, read the dry, sardonic remarks of cynical philosophers like Cioran or even Carl Schmitt, read newspapers, read those who despise, dismiss, or simply ignore poetry and try to understand why they do it. Read your enemies and your friends, read those who reinforce your sense of what's evolving in poetry, and also read those whose darkness or malice or madness or greatness you can't yet understand because only in this way will you grow, outlive yourself, and become what you are.

14 Writing in Polish

People sometimes ask me: "Why don't you write in English?" Or—if I'm in France—why not in French? They clearly assume that I'd benefit, that I'd do better using some universal language instead of my provincial Polish. And I agree in principle; it would certainly be easier to write in some more important language (if I could pull it off!). It reminds me of a story about George Bernard Shaw, who supposedly confessed in a letter to Henryk Sienkiewicz that he couldn't understand why the Poles didn't simply switch to Russian. The Irish had, after all, mastered English and were managing beautifully! Really.

Writing in Polish—in the nineteenth century, after the partitions—was an act of patriotism. The Polish language was in grave danger, especially in the Russian sector. Today it's no longer a question. Even if he remembers his city's past—and such remembrance is in fashion these days—a young poet born in Gdansk won't hesitate in choosing which language to use. He only knows one, after all. Only someone like myself, who's lived abroad for years, meets up with the—naive?—question of picking his language.

Writing in Polish also means accepting the complex legacy of Polish history. Someone who writes French with irony, elegance, and a pinch of poetry inherits, willy-nilly, not just Montaigne and Pascal but also Louis XIV, or at least the atmosphere of his court, with its mocking conversations, murderous bons mots, anxious moralists, and revolutionary demagogues. The Polish writer has different genes in his blood and ink: the state's collapse in the eighteenth century, the defeat inflicted by the partitions, the failed uprisings, and the frailty of our country's long, theatrical existence. Since Poland did not exist in a palpable, pragmatic sense, it became a chimera, subject alternately to admiration (*Polenlieder* in the 1830s, French enthusiasm) and disdain (Bismarck, the German and Russian nationalists). Poland vegetated in the European imagination rather like the charming Tadzio in Mann's *Death in Venice*—beautiful, elusive, ethereal, and childlike. Or just the opposite—it was a dirty, drunken backwater (see, for example, Goethe's description of his brief visit to Poland, commemorated by a plaque in Krakow's main square) to be vanquished as quickly as possible. Beauty or the beast, nothing in between. Poles still listen mistrustfully, but with great curiosity, to the opinions expressed about them in the West's great cities.

Now we come to another key issue—are the Poles the heroes of World War II, splendid uhlans fighting tanks on horseback, bold pilots over England, peerless, patient conspirators, fearless soldiers tackling Monte Cassino? Or are they the primitive anti-Semites with low foreheads portrayed as pigs in a well-known American comic book? Beauty or the beast? Gentlemen or swine? And finally: Did they emerge spotless from communism, rebelling, sabotaging the system forced on them by Moscow? That's how they like to see themselves, at any rate. Or did they also submissively collaborate like all the other captive nations? Poles disagree to this day on the nature of the purgatory they've passed through. One well-known historian published a book a while back called *The Poles' Great Century.* She has in mind precisely the period of political nonexistence, the nineteenth century; and she works from the assumption that the frenetic intellectual activity of the émigrés scattered throughout Europe, poets, thinkers, historians, politicians, more than compensates for our lack of national sovereignty. Can this be true?

Readers scour the scores of memoirs recalling the wartime and postwar years, looking not just for individual fates but for an answer to the question: Who are we? And writers share their anxiety—not just the memoirists but also great literary talents. All Witold Gombrowicz's work fairly vibrates with, among other things, this very worry.

A Western European can imagine the abyss of modern Polish history only with difficulty. There is, for example, the moment—captured on film, no doubt, by some well-fed Wehrmacht cameraman—when Warsaw's surviving population marches in a single resigned, irregular, and endless column made up of men, women, children, and the aged, all abandoning their ruined city in the fall of 1944, after the failed uprising. This scene surely has its place in the all-too-rich collection of the past century's most horrific images. A civilian population meekly deserts its razed city, the capital of a European nation: what could be worse? (Only the camps and crematoria, and the horror of an even more hopeless uprising in the same city's Jewish ghetto in 1943.)

This same moment also became, though, a point of reference for an invisible debate initiated by Polish writers just after the war. Obviously they didn't conduct this discussion like professional historians. They didn't debate the issue of blame and responsibility for the Warsaw Uprising; they didn't analyze the military and political situation. But that zero degree of literature (far more painful here than in Roland Barthes's academic essay), the nothingness that Warsaw, and with it all of Poland, had endured, would color the imagination of Polish writers for years to come. Not just color it; this nothingness became one of its chief ingredients. The Polish literary imagination assimilated the abyss.

It goes without saying that the years of Stalinism brought no fundamental improvement. Of course, the terror was less horrific than it had been under Hitler, and a fair number of Poles shared the conviction that rebuilding the country, even under the Communist Party's brutal direction, was a praiseworthy undertaking that couldn't wait for better days. But few were free of deep bitterness. The communist economy's grotesque wastefulness and the ubiquitous secret police were a constant reminder that this enterprise was closer to the theater of the absurd than to rational government policy.

Time's relentless, redemptive frivolity means that the present young generation, well versed in postmodern theory and the pitfalls of the text, has already forgotten that horror. But the radicality of postwar Polish literature owes much to the energetic response to that moment, the moment when Warsaw's population abandoned its devastated city. Today's literary debutants can of course remember nothing, but even for me and my contemporaries, born just after the war, the shattered buildings overgrown with grass were as seductive as the ruins of a Gothic abbey had been for the first generation of Romantics. They concealed both treasures and dangers, they were the natural, cherished landscape of our childhood, our first inspiration.

In the Poland of the last sixty years—in Poland itself, but also in emigration since, as every schoolchild in Krakow knows, Polish literature took shape in Paris, Argentina, California as much as at home—writing was rarely an academic, cerebral, bloodless, marginal occupation. It seldom led to a personal quest for Beauty, to Flaubertian tussles with language, to the scrupulous recording of a single, singular life story. It was more like a blazing, roaring kiln in which—at high temperatures and before the eyes of eager witnesses, inquisitive members of the polis—the vessels of poetry and prose were fired. Writing carried enormous weight, it was a great and serious debate in which existential worries met with problems touching the whole society, the whole polis. At the same time, paradoxically, the participants in this debate—Witold Gombrowicz, Jerzy Stempowski, Czeslaw Milosz, Aleksander Wat, Jozef Czapski, Zbigniew Herbert, Gustaw Herling-Grudzinski, to name just a few titans—rebelled, rejected it. They hungered for the great, universal subjects and ideas, they yearned for metaphysics—but they could achieve these only by laboriously hacking a path through the jungle of questions springing from the social and political terrain. They all wrote wonderfully, needless to say: we're dealing not with a group of ideologues but with great writers, masters of the word.

Polish literature can only be understood against this background. This obviously wasn't the literature of noblemen, as in previous ages, sitting comfortably on their estates or at court, reading Plutarch and Virgil and then, after successfully gathering the fruits of their labors, sitting down to unhurried literary creation. The generation whose maturity coincided with the moment of the great crisis, the great Nothing, was scattered across the globe and fought to survive in circumstances that were unimaginably difficult, both materially and spiritually; they were despised by the leftists, Parisian and otherwise. But they managed to create the basis for a new literary sensibility in Poland. They forged a literature that answered history's menace in universal, not provincial, ways. And they touched profound hopes while shunning easy consolations.

The dilemma of writers from behind the Iron Curtain is well illustrated by a quote from the recently, posthumously published diaries of the writer and composer Zygmunt Mycielski (*Diary, 1950–59*): "In the West I would doubtlessly have been a 'dark writer,' someone whose puffings on the tuba of pessimism would have foretold the fall of Europe and the world and preached the absurdity of human progress and our species' evolution. Over here, on the ragheap of economies and ideas, I blow the trumpet of morality and the meaning of existence."

The major role Polish poets play in matters usually consigned to novelists or even philosophers is conspicuous. Polish poets never accepted modernism's ascetic dictates; they refused to retreat to a sanctuary of hermetic metaphors. They chose instead to study the world's ailments with great vigor; and judging by the interest their work inspired, it was a good choice. Students read Milosz's *Treatise on Poetry* beneath their desktops during Stalinism's worst years. Adam Wazyk's *Poem for Grownups*, published in 1955, sparked a nationwide discussion and led to the success of the post-Stalinist political thaw. Zbigniew Herbert wrote his poem "The Envoy of Mr. Cogito" in despair; he foresaw no hope of change, no end to despotism. But the poem itself became something of an anthem, recited by the opposition throughout the seventies and eighties. And these poets managed to reach a wider public with their artistic standards intact!

I'm convinced that writing in Polish would be far more difficult today without this generation of titans. Their very greatness and nobility may have created another problem, though. Their literary inheritors have been unable to play out the customary Oedipal comedy, the comic war of generations, the ritual burning of the father's portrait. How do you rebel against truth's martyrs, the magnificent, gifted witnesses to their age?

There's yet another problem. That generation wrote in some sense "from ideas," quarreling and contending with ideology, desperately defending endangered humanity. It was thus forced to focus on the intellectual articulation of reality and ignored the potentially endless number of human situations created not by hostile outside forces, but by the innate, implacable mutability of the world itself.

And there's a third problem. Its furious polemics with recent history meant that Polish literature couldn't do justice to something we might call the "pure," "ahistorical" imagination. It's true that some writers of that generation, Aleksander Wat or Czeslaw Milosz, recognized this difficulty and spoke more than once of poetry's need to strive for the ontological strata of being, or, more simply put, the now-unfashionable (and essential) question of religion.

Writing in Polish: ever-changing threats confront anyone who risks it. The celebrated "normalcy," so difficult to define, that Eastern Europe's inhabitants had longed for, finally prevailed in literature as well as life. Frivolity is now permitted; you may now write easily, superficially, and rather gracefully about yourself and others (most often yourself). The great, rather haphazard victory of democracy over totalitarianism may also appear to be the triumph of banality over lies: lies are the heart of totalitarianism, while democracy shields no one from vulgarity.

Although they may not realize it, Polish writers of the middle and younger generation still walk beneath the umbrella raised for them by the titans. In literature, though, this umbrella not only fends off rain; it also screens the starry sky. It's not clear how long such protection will suffice.

Writing in Polish—but does it finally matter what language we write in? Can't any language, properly used, open the road to poetry, the world? The writer ordinarily sits alone with a blank piece of paper or a pale computer screen staring boldly and intently back at him. He's alone although he doesn't write for himself, but for others. Inspired and impeded by tradition, that great tumult of dead voices, he struggles to see into the future, which is always mute. The thoughts he hopes to express seem at times not to be part of any language; they roar within him like another element, alongside air, water, and fire.

He's alone; he voices joy or sorrow. His quest's witnesses are neither passport offices nor university grammarians, but sun and death, two forces, as La Rochefoucauld said, we can't look in the face.